Mosdos Press
Literature
Opal

Student Activity Workbook

Companion to

DAISY

Mosdos Press
CLEVELAND, OHIO

Editor-in-Chief
Judith Factor

Creative/Art Director
Carla Martin

Senior Curriculum Writer
Abigail Rozen

Copy Editor
Laya Dewick

Text and Curriculum Advisor
Rabbi Ahron Dovid Goldberg

ISBN-10: 0-9858078-7-3
ISBN-13: 978-0-985-80787-0

Table of Contents

UNIT 4
All About Setting!

UNIT 5
All About Theme!

UNIT 6
The Grand Finalé!

cyclones   enable
transport   harsh
ambition   primary
briefly   theory

Fill in the blanks.

1. Clyde was a "storm chaser." That means he was a person who traveled to places where storms were predicted. He traveled far and wide to experience hurricanes, tornadoes, and _____ (*a storm in which the wind blows in circles*).

2. He would pack up and _____ (*move*) all the equipment he needed to survive the storm: flashlights, water, rain gear, canned food, and so on.

3. He came prepared for the most difficult, _____ (*rough and unpleasant*) conditions. Rain, wind, cold, and lack of electricity did not scare him.

4. He sometimes called the mayor of the town that he was about to visit to ask for any help that would _____ (*make it possible*) him to experience the coming storm.

5. His dream, his goal, his _____ (*goal*) was to make pictures and videos of every kind of storm known to man.

6. Sometimes, a storm came earlier than predicted. He would travel to the place, even if he knew he would be there only _____ (*for a short time*).

7. His main, _____ (*most important*) goal was to record every different type of stormy weather.

8. You see, he had his own ideas and _____ (*unproven idea*) about storm patterns. He wanted to prove them and then write a book telling the world how to better predict and prepare for them. But secretly, he found them thrilling, and he just loved being right in the middle of the wind and the rain!

True or False

Some of these statements are true and some of them are false. Write a T or an F in front of each sentence.

1. _____ If you want a wonderful, relaxing vacation, you should make sure to be in a place where the weather is **harsh**.

2. _____ When you give the **primary** reason for doing something, you are saying that it is a small, unimportant part of why you are doing it.

3. _____ You don't have to believe a **theory**, because it is something that has not been proven.

4. _____ During a **cyclone**, the wind blows in a huge circle.

5. _____ People with **ambitions** have no dreams or goals.

6. _____ Airplanes are often used to **transport** mail.

7. _____ Getting enough sleep will **enable** you to think clearly.

8. _____ After listening to a speaker drone on for more than an hour, you may wonder why the speaker speaks so **briefly**.

Your Move

MOVING

The Town That Moved did not move very far. But people all over America move all the time! Some move down the block and some move halfway across the country. If you could move to any place at all, where would it be? What would it look like? What weather would it have? Would it be near the water or high on a hill? Write two paragraphs about the place you would move to and why you would choose it.

_____

_____

_____

_____

_____

_____

_____

_____

_____

_____

_____

_____

_____

_____

_____

Cause and Effect

All day, every day, you experience **cause and effect**. Was it dark when you got up this morning? You probably turned on the light. You pressed a button—that was the *cause*. The light went on—that was the *effect*. Then, you made some noise, and the baby woke up. You made some noise—that was the *cause*. The baby woke up—that was the *effect*.

In the following sentences, underline the cause, and circle the effect. Remember that in a sentence, sometimes the cause is first, and sometimes the effect is first. The first one is done for you.

1. Mr. Jenkins pressed the elevator button. The elevator doors opened immediately, and he stepped inside.

2. I was sound asleep when that noisy alarm went off. Why, I almost jumped out of my skin!

3. The doe sensed danger. She nudged her young fawn, and the two fled into the woods.

4. We were having a great time batting the balloons around when one of the balloons hit a hot light bulb and burst with a bang.

5. "What happened to you?" asked Helen. "Well," said Andrea, "I fell down the steps and sprained my ankle."

6. Little Lonnie's mouth was bright purple. She was licking a purple Popsicle which was slowly melting onto her overalls.

In *The Town That Moved*, an entire town is moved from one place to another. Just for fun, we are going to help you "move" some parts of a town, too! To move the hotel, animal, and tractor from "old Hibbing" to "new Hibbing," copy each line of pictures on this page into the blank frames on the next page.

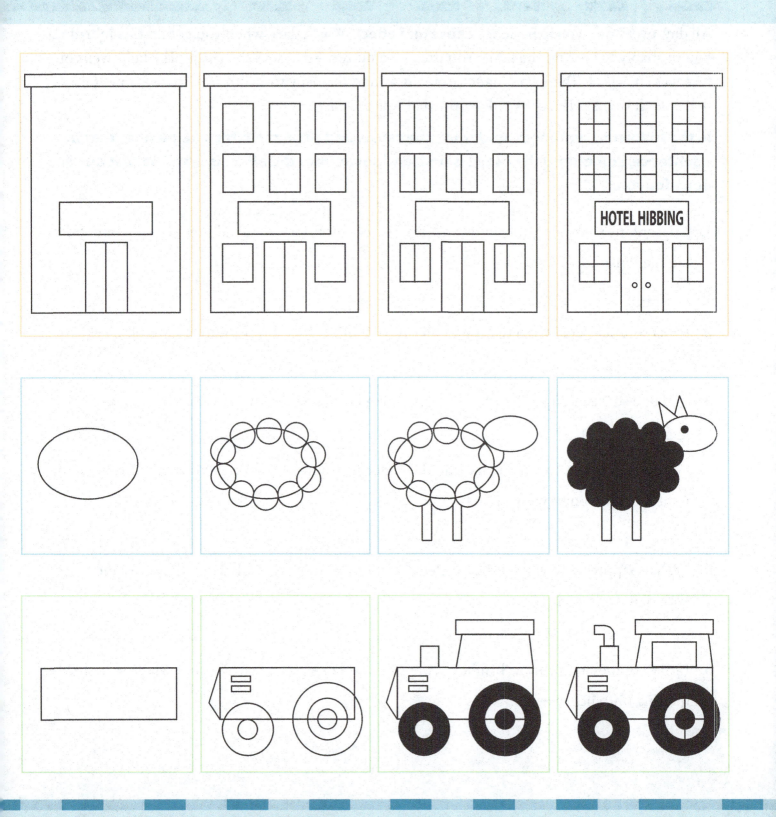

Name

You Draw It!

fertile	weathered
hues	define
livestock	merged
toil	drought

Fill in the blanks.

1. What if our soil were not rich and _____ (*allowing plants to grow easily*)?

2. What if the sky at sunset were not a rainbow of _____ (*colors*)?

3. What if our _____ (*farm animals*) were poor and sickly?

4. What if _____ (*lack of rain*) and dryness were everywhere in the news?

5. What if _____ (*roughened by the weather*) farmers said they would stop planting?

6. What if they just said, we will not _____ (*work very hard*)?

7. What if they _____ (*joined*) their voices saying, "We're retiring!"

8. What if they were not all so loyal? Let us explain our emotions, let us _____ (*explain*) how we feel. We are grateful for all of these blessings. Our appreciation is deep, great, and real.

If ...

Circle the correct answer.

1. If your uncle owns **livestock**, he is probably a

   a. businessman.   b. farmer.

   _____

2. If there is a **drought** in your neighborhood, your grass is probably

   a. green.   b. brown.

   _____

3. If two roads **merge**,

   a. they turn into one road.   b. they turn into three roads.

   _____

4. If you like things with many **hues**, you will probably like

   a. rainbows.   b. music.

   _____

5. If your teacher asks you to **define** a word, you may need

   a. a clear speaking voice.   b. a dictionary.

   _____

6. If a man's face looks **weathered** to you,

   a. he has rough, lined skin.   b. you have probably met him before.

   _____

7. If the soil in your backyard is **fertile**,

   a. it is a good place for a rock garden.   b. it is a good place for a vegetable garden.

   _____

8. If your day has been full of **toil**,

   a. you need some rest.   b. you need some advice.

Write Ten Details

Most of us look around us, but hardly notice what we are seeing. An artist who wishes to paint a scene must look carefully at every detail that makes up the scene. Choose a scene that you see often. It may be your own backyard, or a group of buildings on a main street. Look closely at the scene and write a list of ten details that you notice. You could include details like: "a bird is hopping on the lawn"; "the weeds look greener than the grass"; "the bricks look old and crumbly." Try to see things that you never noticed before.

SEEING

_____

_____

_____

_____

_____

_____

_____

_____

_____

_____

Recognizing Rhyme

Rhyming words sound alike. But there is more to rhyming words than just matching the sounds. A good rhyme will have the *same number of syllables* in the rhyming words. One-syllable words like "Sam," will rhyme with "am" and "yam." Two-syllable words like "bubble," will rhyme with "double" and "trouble." The words will rhyme as exactly as possible.

Circle the best answer.

1. What rhymes best with *pop*?

   pip   top   rope   pot

2. What rhymes best with *table*?

   marble   fable   maple   tail

3. What rhymes best with *mixer*?

   fiction   boxer   picker   fixer

4. What rhymes best with *addition*?

   fiction   tradition   fishin'   dishes

5. What rhymes best with *chicken*?

   linen   blacken   children   thicken

6. What rhymes best with *fairly*?

   scary   early   merrily   rarely

7. What rhymes best with *mess*?

   less   nest   arrest   met

8. What rhymes best with *money*?

   mummy   funny   monkey   muddy

Heartland is a poem, but it could be a picture book. It describes scene after scene in beautiful words. In the following exercise, you will be the illustrator of this poem. Opposite the words in each box, draw a picture that the words describe. Pay special attention to the colors mentioned.

1.

I am the land where wheat fields grow

In golden waves that ebb and flow;

Where cornfields stretched across the plains

Lie green between the country lanes.

2.

A patchwork quilt laid gently down

In hues of yellow, green, and brown

As tractors, plows, and planters go

Across my fields . . .

Illustrate a Poem!

3.

And neon-lighted shadows fall

From windowed walls of brick that rise

Toward the clouds, to scrape the skies;

4.

And winter, white and cold, descends

With blizzards howling as they sweep

Across me, piling snowdrifts deep

carousel	insistently
circumference	speculate
debating	tufts
gawking	wafted

Fill in the blanks.

1. As children, my brother and I would spend hours discussing amusement park rides, arguing and _____ (*arguing back and forth*) the pros and cons of each one.

2. "The only *real* ride is the roller coaster!" my brother would say _____ (*without a letup*).

3. I would shudder, imagining everyone _____ (*staring*) at me as I shrieked louder than anyone else on the roller coaster.

4. My brother would _____ (*suggest possible reasons*) about what frightened me about roller coasters. "I guess you're afraid of heights," he would say.

5. He was right, but I also didn't like any ride that was too fast, too dark, or too weird. The only ride for me was a slow-moving _____ (*merry-go-round*) with pretty horses that went up and down a pole.

6. The pretty gate that went around the _____ (*border of a circle*) of the platform made me feel safe.

7. I liked to stroke the _____ (*cottony bunches*) of "horse hair" that were glued to the shiny wooden horses. "You are such a baby!" my brother would tease. "Am not!" I would answer.

8. But there was one spot at the amusement park we both loved. It was a small building from which the delicious smell of hot popcorn _____ (*floated through the air*), filling the summer air with glorious smells.

Definitions

Laughing Sal has a real funny bone. When someone uses a word the wrong way, she laughs until she's red in the face! Below, you will find words with two possible definitions. One is the correct definition and one—well, it's so wrong that Laughing Sal finds it hilarious.

Circle the definition that will *not* make Sal laugh (the correct one)!

1. Is a **carousel**

    a. a merry-go-round   **or**   b. a small suitcase?

    _____

2. Is a **circumference**

    a. a meeting of important people **or**   b. the border of a circle?

    _____

3. Is **debating**

    a. arguing   **or**   b. preparing your fishing line with worms?

    _____

4. Is **gawking**

    a. hunting predatory birds   **or**   b. staring?

    _____

5. Does **insistently** mean

    a. without a letup   **or**   b. immediately?

    _____

6. To **speculate** may mean

    a. to get fitted for glasses   **or**   b. to suggest a possible reason.

    _____

7. Are **tufts**

    a. cottony bunches   **or**   b. very strong cloths?

    _____

8. If something has **wafted**, is it

    a. an aroma   **or**   b. twisted and knotted?

A Home Run—
or a Broken Window?

C
R
A
S
H
!

One boring afternoon, Caroline and Earl compete to see who can hit a ball farther. When Caroline steps up to the plate, the only thing on her mind is hitting the ball farther than Earl did. The next thing she knows, her ball has broken Mrs. Williams' window.

Has this ever happened to you? You start out with great plans to do something wonderful and suddenly, everything changes. Write a story about plans that got ruined by some unexpected event. Your story may have a sad or disappointing ending, or, you might wish to show how everything turned out for the best. Even better, you may tell the story in a way that turns "tragedy" into "comedy" and gets your reader to laugh!

_____

_____

_____

_____

_____

_____

_____

_____

_____

_____

Setting

Setting is when and where a story takes place. When you read, you "go" to that time and place in your imagination.

What is the setting of the following paragraphs? Circle the correct answer in each set.

1. Livi was the youngest of eight children. They lived on an island in the South Pacific. The days were warm and sunny. She and her brothers and sisters helped their parents fish and garden. When they had free time, the children would splash in the warm waves or play in the nearby forest.

    a. a small school   b. a great forest   c. a warm island

2. The fawn trotted quickly after the two big deer. The woods were getting darker, and the little fawn had strayed from its mother. He was hungry and afraid of the dark. He hoped that the big deer would lead him to his mother. As big snowflakes began to fall, he saw a doe in the distance. Was that his mother?

    a. a city zoo   b. a dark woods   c. a hot jungle

3. The subway was hot and crowded. Jason hung onto the back of someone's seat to keep from falling as the subway shook and rattled its way through the tunnel. Outside, the big city was hotter than the subway car. Jason thought about the job he was trying out for in the big skyscraper in Manhattan. He wondered if they would hire him.

    a. a skyscraper in Manhattan   b. the streets of New York   c. a crowded subway

4. Brenda looked around the emergency room. Sitting across from her were a mother and her little boy. The little boy had fallen asleep. Brenda wondered who was sick, the mother or the boy. Next to them was a young man with his leg up on a chair. He looked like he was in a lot of pain but was joking with his friend. Maybe he broke his leg skiing, thought Brenda. Brenda's wrist began to throb. She had fallen off a ladder, and her wrist had blown up like a balloon.

    a. the school gym   b. a hospital emergency room   c. a hill where people are skiing

Emotions are feelings, like happiness, anger, or jealousy. In a good story, the characters experience many different emotions. As we read, we can tell how the character is feeling by what is happening in the story. In each car of the roller coaster below, you will see a quote from the story. How does the character feel at that moment? Choose one emotion from the list and write it into the track under the car.

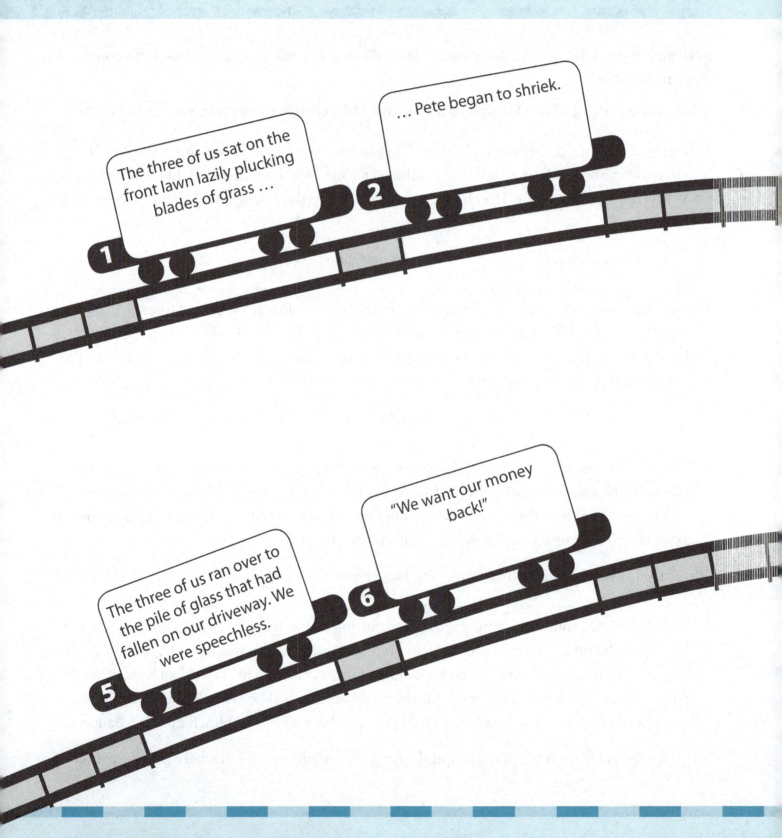

Identifying Emotions

bored   angry
irritated   happy
surprised   worried
grateful   frightened

3 "What's all that racket?" called my father from inside the house.

4 A little voice in the back of my mind told me that our driveway was very close to Mrs. Williams' house.

7 A little smile crossed her face, then it grew … and grew …

8 "I'm paying a dollar, but really, what you've given me, Peter, is priceless."

molasses	enormous
craving	rivets
clattered	rumbling
cobblestones	chaos

Fill in the blanks.

1. This was the problem: our dog was just too fat. In fact, he was _____ (*huge*)!

2. We had gotten him when he was just a puppy. He was always busily digging around in our backyard, so we named him Beaver. It was only later that we realized that he was digging for food! His stomach always seemed to be _____ (*making a deep low noise*).

3. He loved all food, but he especially had a _____ (*desire*) for sweets.

4. We had a metal box, held together with _____ (*metal pins*) in which we locked up any open jar or box of sweets.

5. One time, my mother was baking cookies, and she had a jar of _____ (*a thick brown syrup*) in a bag on the counter.

6. When she left the kitchen for a moment, Beaver quickly climbed onto the counter, grabbed the bag in his mouth, and dragged it out onto our street, which is paved with old-fashioned _____ (*stones used for paving streets*).

7. I heard the jar as it _____ (*made a loud sound*) on the stones, but it was too late!

8. The jar broke, the molasses ran all over the street, and cars, trying to swerve around the broken glass and fat little dog, created confusion and _____ (*confusion*).

Is/Are ...?

Circle the correct answer.

1. Is **molasses**

    a. a type of fish   **or**   b. a kind of syrup?

2. Are **cobblestones** used

    a. to build houses   **or**   b. to pave roads?

3. Is **rumbling**

    a. a deep, low sound   **or**   b. a high screechy sound?

4. Is **chaos**

    a. very confusing   **or**   b. very orderly?

5. Are **rivets** used

    a. to hold hair in place   **or**   b. to hold metal together?

6. Is a **craving**

    a. a strong desire for a certain thing   **or**   b. a strong fear of a certain thing?

7. Is something **enormous**

    a. very small   **or**   b. very big?

8. Is something that **clatters**

    a. full of rattling sounds   **or**   b. a tool that cuts metal?

Misunderstood

TRUTH

When Patrick told his mother what had happened to him, she accused him of making up the story. Have you ever had the experience of being misunderstood? Did you ever tell the truth, but were told you must be telling a lie? Were you able to prove that you *were* telling the truth? Write two paragraphs about a time when you were misunderstood, and what you did about it. If you or someone you know has never had this kind of an experience, you may make up a story about someone who did.

_____

_____

_____

_____

_____

_____

_____

_____

_____

_____

_____

_____

_____

_____

Name _____

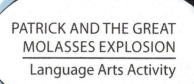

Visualizing

Do you know what the most powerful part of you is? No, it's not your arm or your leg. It's your imagination! When we read or hear stories, we use our imaginations to **visualize** what is being described. The better the story, the easier it is for us to picture what is happening in the story.

Match the pictures to the words that describe them.

1. _____ The lion stood at the peak of the hill and roared.

   _____

2. _____ When we woke up, the entire world seemed to be covered with snow, like a huge, frosted cake.

   _____

3. _____ Just as we turned the corner, another car bumped into ours. Crash! Luckily, both cars were going slowly, so only the fenders got dented.

   _____

4. _____ There goes old Mr. Murtell, walking down the street. He always stands so straight and walks so quickly, you would think he was a young man of twenty.

   _____

5. _____ We stood outside my favorite place, the library. It was an old building, with ivy climbing up the dark stone walls.

4   **1**   **5**   **3**   **2**

PATRICK AND THE GREAT MOLASSES EXPLOSION

Graphic Organizer

Every story has a beginning, a middle, and an end. In the beginning, the background is given. In the middle, the main action takes place. In the end, the problems are solved and the action is completed.

The following exercise teaches you to outline a story by summarizing the beginning, middle, and end of *Patrick and the Great Molasses Explosion*. Complete each statement by writing the answer on the line. You may look at the list of scrambled answers and choose the correct one.

The Beginning

1. This story is about a boy named _____.

2. Patrick loved to eat _____.

3. Patrick and his family lived in the city of _____.

4. Every Sunday Patrick and Papa took a walk along the _____.

• •

The Middle

1. One day, Mama sent Patrick to the corner store to buy _____.

2. The store was out of molasses, so Patrick decided to go to another _____.

3. Just as he arrived at the second store, Patrick heard a loud _____!

4. Rushing to the corner, Patrick saw a towering _____ of molasses coming down the street.

• •

The End

1. When Patrick told his mother what had happened, she did not _____ him.

2. Because he was so sticky, she made him take a _____.

3. Then, because she thought he was lying, she made him go to _____.

4. When he woke up, Patrick tried to tell his mother the _____, but she still did not believe him.

Outlining a Story

5. Patrick's favorite sight at the harbor was a huge tank with the following words painted on it:

   _____ Distilling Company.

6. The tank was full of _____.

bahror   tipcark
sobnot   sosmales
somassle   riputy

5. Patrick grabbed his pail, filled it with molasses, and _____.

6. When he fell, a man came and _____ him up.

7. Patrick walked slowly home, _____ molasses along the way.

rotes   ombo
ginlick   depcik
nar   avew
soasmsle

5. Mama finally heard the story when _____ came home.

6. Mama felt so bad that she offered Patrick a lot of _____.

7. For the first time, Patrick _____.

tahb   deb
appa   somassle
dusefer   thurt
elibeve

telltale	hibernation
intent	burrowed
skimmed	darted
talons	dodge

Fill in the blanks.

1. It was spring at the North Pole. Anyone could see it; the _____
   (*something that tells a secret*) signs were there.

2. The ice was beginning to thaw. Some of the animals who had _____
   (*dug a hole to live in*) deep in the ground were beginning to come out of their holes.

3. If one looked, one could see some big birds as they _____ (*passed
   lightly over*) along the shoreline, looking for fish or some small animal they could eat.

4. Sometimes you could see them sailing through the air with some small animal in their
   _____ (*claws*).

5. If you stood near one of the many streams, you could see the fish as they
   _____ (*started suddenly and ran*) through the icy water.

6. You might see a big bear, just out of _____ (*sleeping through the
   winter*), lumbering along, looking for food.

7. In fact, almost any animal you would see would be _____ on
   (*determined to*) finding something to eat.

8. At the same time, most of the animals had to _____ (*avoid*) other
   animals to avoid being *their* dinner.

Name _____

Mixed Up Molly

Meet Mixed Up Molly! Molly knows a lot of words, but sometimes gets a little mixed up about what the words mean. Can you help her learn the real meaning of these words?

Write your answer on the line.

1. Molly thinks **burrowed** describes something that your friend has loaned you. It doesn't!

    It means _____

    _____

2. Molly thinks **telltale** describes how a dog lets you know when he's really happy! It doesn't!

    It means _____

    _____

3. Molly thinks **hibernation** is a large group of people called the "Hibers." It's not!

    It's _____

    _____

4. Molly thinks that **skimmed** describes something that's had its skin taken off. It doesn't!

    It means _____

    _____

5. Molly thinks that **intent** is where you sleep when you're on a camping trip. It's not!

    It's _____

    _____

6. Molly thinks that **talons** are special abilities, like singing well or drawing well. They're not!

    They're _____

    _____

7. Molly thinks that **darted** means throwing little arrows at a board. It doesn't!

    It means _____

    _____

8. Molly thinks **dodged** means—well, she's not sure *what* it means, because a Dodge is a make of car, but she knows *that's* not what the word means! What *does* it mean?

    It means _____

An Animal Story

ANIMALS

Bear Mouse tells the story of how a very hungry mouse searches for food in the winter. Choose a bird, fish, or animal and write two paragraphs about its search for food. In the first paragraph, write about what it usually eats and why it doesn't have food now. In the second paragraph, write about where and how it searches for food.

_____

_____

_____

_____

_____

_____

_____

_____

_____

_____

_____

_____

_____

_____

Descriptive Words

To help the reader visualize the story, a writer uses **descriptive** words. A descriptive word *describes* something. It may describe the way something *looks*, like a *red* ball. It may describe the way something *feels*, like *soft* wool. It may describe the way something *sounds*, like *loud* music. Descriptive words can describe objects, people, and feelings—anything in the world!

Choose the descriptive word that best fits and write it on the line in the sentence.

1. The _____ mouse stood still, only her nose twitching. She listened. She looked. She sensed danger.

   hungry   frightened
   happy   brown

2. The _____ sun beat down on our backs. I was scared. Were we lost in the desert?

   warm   weak
   hot   setting

3. I just love going to the zoo. Every animal is different and _____. Did I mention that I love cotton candy, too?

   boring   interesting
   scary   lazy

4. I shut my eyes tight. I heard the nurse say, "This won't hurt," and felt the _____ needle go into my arm.

   little   sharp
   soft   red

5. As we went deeper and deeper underground, the air felt _____. That was probably because there was water running down the walls of the cave.

   cold   dry
   heavy   damp

6. There it was—the gift I had hoped for ... a _____ two-wheeler that was just the right size for me!

   old   red
   bent   slow

It was winter and Bear Mouse had to feed her babies. But how was she to find food for them? Wherever she searched, there were enemies trying to eat *her*. And, even when she escaped them, she couldn't find food. Here and there, she found a berry or a seed, until the end, when she found a hidden store of seeds and acorns. Follow the little mouse as she goes from place to place.

The meadow (food)

A cocoon

Turtle Pond

A red berry

The alder bush

A covering of ice

The meadow (enemy)

A hawk

Name

Draw a line between each place and what she found there.

The meadow

High in the pine tree

The stone wall

The crack between the stones

The bobcat

A lot of seeds and acorns

The cardinal

The snowy owl

flickered   frail

fringe   schedule

confessed   wisdom

fierce   determination

Fill in the blanks.

1. I was right on _____ (*a plan to do certain things at certain times*) for my visit to the nursing home.

2. Even though it was a snowy day, my _____ (*the strong will to do something*) showed as I stomped through the slush on the sidewalk.

3. In the morning I _____ (*admitted*) to a friend that I would have liked to put off my visit.

4. When I finally got to my great aunt's room and saw the light of the scented candle I had given her as it _____ (*shone with a wavering light*) through the window, I knew I had done the right thing.

5. My kind aunt sat in her rocking chair wrapped in her favorite shawl with the blue _____ (*a border of loose threads*) all around it.

6. She looked very _____ (*weak*) but I knew that the way she looked had nothing to do with her kind and welcoming ways.

7. The _____ (*strong and wild*) wind was blowing outside, but in my aunt's lovely room everything was calm and peaceful.

8. I had an important problem to discuss with my favorite great-aunt and I was sure her common sense and _____ (*intelligence and understanding*) would really be very helpful.

How Are These Words Used?

Circle the correct answer.

1. What **flickers**?

   a. A dog's tail   b. A candle

   _____

2. What has a **fringe**?

   a. A sea lion   b. A shawl

   _____

3. Who might **confess**?

   a. One who has done wrong   b. One who has done the right thing

   _____

4. What causes **determination**?

   a. A lack of vitamins   b. A strong will

   _____

5. Which is **fierce**?

   a. A lion   b. A lamb

   _____

6. Which is **frail**?

   a. An old woman   b. A young boxer

   _____

7. When is a train on **schedule**?

   a. When it arrives on time   b. When it arrives late

   _____

8. What is **wisdom**?

   a. A type of stone   b. A type of intelligence

A Gift

Sometimes a gift is just something nice that could have been given to any number of people. But sometimes, a gift is more than just nice; it has special meaning to the person who is giving it and the person who is receiving it. It says, "I care about you and understand you." Choose someone that you care about. Think of a gift that says, "I have chosen a gift just for you." The gift doesn't even have to be an object. It could be a visit, a lesson, or a phone call. Describe the gift and the person you are giving it to. Explain why this gift would be especially meaningful to that person.

_____

_____

_____

_____

_____

_____

_____

_____

_____

_____

_____

C
A
R
I
N
G

Drawing Conclusions

Drawing a conclusion is like solving a problem in addition. As a matter of fact, when someone draws a conclusion, that person will often say, "I put two and two together."

In the following exercise, two sentences are presented in the form of an addition problem. What conclusion do you come to when you have read the sentences?

Circle the best answer.

1. Ryan walks his dog every morning. **+** This morning, Ryan's father is walking the dog.

    a. Ryan loves dogs.

    b. Ryan is either sick or out of town.

    c. You just never know when Ryan will surprise you.

2. Ginny walked up the steps, knocked lightly at the door, and waited. **+** Ginny's mother opened the door and gasped. A look of surprise crossed her face.

    a. Ginny was not expecting to find her mother at home.

    b. Ginny's mother was very happy that Ginny had come home.

    c. Ginny's mother was not expecting to see Ginny at this time.

3. Cary the Clown looked in the mirror. **+** "How on earth will I entertain the children today?" he thought. "I'll just have to paint that smile bigger and brighter than usual," he told himself.

    a. Cary the Clown is unhappy for some reason.

    b. Cary the Clown is in a great hurry, but still takes a minute to look in the mirror.

    c. Cary the Clown feels happier than usual today, and the mirror tells him so.

4. "Goodbye," I shouted happily to my father as I raced out the door. **+** "Goodbye," my father signed to me, as he smiled and waved.

    a. The father is hearing impaired, and his son loves him.

    b. The son is annoyed that his father cannot hear him and is happy to leave the house.

    c. The son is angry that his father is making him go somewhere he doesn't want to go.

A GIFT FOR TIA ROSA
Graphic Organizer

A gift is anything given by one person to another as an expression of love or friendship. A gift does not even have to be an object. It can be a friendly wave or a warm hello. *A Gift for Tía Rosa* is about many kinds of gifts, although you may not have thought of them all as gifts. Every person in the story gave something to somebody else. Select the correct "gift" and copy it into the empty gift box in each picture.

Tío Juan to Carmela

Tía Rosa to Carmela

Carmela to Tía Rosa

Carmela to Tío Juan

he was a good listener

she made him smile

she showed her how much she loved her

she taught her to knit

Name

Carmela to Tía Rosa

Carmela's father to Carmela

Tía Rosa to Carmela

Carmela's mother to Carmela

she gave her good advice

she visited her every day

he comforted Carmela

she gave her a necklace

impoverished	hardship
graceful	swiftly
sensitive	shabby
coward	flexible

Fill in the blanks.

1. As I walked along the street, I saw a man walking _____ (*quickly*) down the street.

2. Although he was wearing old, _____ (*worn out*) clothes, there was something alive about him.

3. This man, I thought, may not have money, but he is not _____ (*poor*). He seems happy and energetic.

4. What was it about him? I wondered. I am a person who is very _____ (*careful about others' feelings*) to others, and seeing him made me curious.

5. As he got nearer to me, I wondered if he had suffered a _____ (*suffering*) recently, which would explain why he looked so poor.

6. My schedule was _____ (*easily changed*), so I decided to slow down and do something I don't usually do.

7. I caught the man's eye just as he was passing and said, "Hello." He answered me with a _____ (*moving in a smooth way*) bow and a bright smile.

8. "How do you do?" he said. "I can see you are no _____ (*one who is fearful*) if you are willing to greet a total stranger."

    "Well," I said, "if I greet you and you greet me, we're not strangers anymore, are we?"

    "Absolutely not! We're friends—and one can never have too many of those."

Name _____

HARLEQUIN AND THE
GIFT OF MANY COLORS
Vocabulary—Activity Two

Remember Backwards Benny? He's the fellow who gets everything backwards. He wears boots to the beach! He eats hamburgers for breakfast! He turns the light on when he goes to sleep! Can you help him out?

Choose the correct word from your vocabulary list on page 38. It will be the opposite of what Benny has said.

1. When Benny saw someone in tattered clothes going into an old house, he said, "That man must be *wealthy*." What he meant to say was, "The man is _____."

2. Benny walked into the dry cleaners, hoping that they would clean his coat in one day. "Can you do the job *slowly*?" he asked. What he meant to say was, "Can you do the job _____?"

3. Benny heard a story about people who suffered during the war. "They lived through *many good times*," he said. He meant to say that they'd lived through much _____.

4. At the zoo, Benny watched the gazelles moving almost like dancers. "They are so delicate and *clumsy*," he said. What he meant to say was, "They are so _____."

5. When they called Benny's name at the dentist's office, he didn't want to go in. "I'm just too *brave*," he said. "Dentists frighten me!" Benny didn't mean he was brave—he meant he was a _____ when it comes to dentists!

6. Although he is not very good at vocabulary, Benny is a very nice person. He will tell you that he cares about the feelings of others. He says, "I can be very *offensive*." But he's *not* offensive! He really is _____.

7. "Please, Mom," said Benny one day. "Could you take me to buy a new coat? The one I'm wearing is *in very good shape*." Luckily, Benny's mother was used to his way of talking, and knew that he meant to say that his coat looked _____.

Helping

Harlequin's friends all worked together to help him. Imagine that one of your friends got sick a short while ago. Although your friend is getting better, it will be many weeks before he or she can go back to school. Your friend is very afraid of falling behind in the classwork, and of missing all the activities in school. You and your friends want to help. Write out a plan that explains how each of you will do something to help your sick classmate keep up with the class. Don't forget that someone at home also needs cheering up, visiting, and a feeling that he or she is still part of the group.

FRIENDS

_____

_____

_____

_____

_____

_____

_____

_____

_____

Summarizing

Summarizing means writing a short version of a story. A summary repeats the main points of the story but *leaves out* its less important points.

Read the following story.

Jeff was a policeman. He was six feet tall and had red hair. Every day, he walked up and down the streets of his town to make sure everything was in order. He knew pretty much everyone in the town, and greeted people with a cheerful "How's it going?" He knew the little girls in their school uniforms and the high school boys who always bounced a basketball on the way to and from school. He knew the little lady with the straw hat and the old man with the cane. He knew the garbage men and the mailmen.

One day, he passed someone he did not know. The man was wearing a big yellow hat and walking a monkey on a leash. Jeff stopped in his tracks. "Who was that?" he thought to himself. That man was so familiar, yet he couldn't place him. It was such a strange feeling, knowing someone and not knowing him at the same time. Was the man dangerous? Should he be followed? Jeff took off his policeman's hat and scratched his head. (Sometimes, that helped him remember things.) He pulled out his little notebook and looked through it to see if he'd ever made a note about a man in a yellow hat.

When he got home, he told his wife and kids about the mysterious stranger. Guess what! They knew who he was! Do YOU?

If you were writing a summary of the story, which details could you leave out? On the lines, write five phrases from the story that you would *not* include in a summary.

1. _____

2. _____

3. _____

4. _____

5. _____

Harlequin and the Gift of Many Colors can be divided into three parts. Each part has its own special problem, its own solution, its own setting, and its own group of characters. Each of the three figures on these pages represents one part of the story. Look at the three piles of patches. Into each figure, write the number of the patch that belongs to that part of the story. Three of them have been done for you.

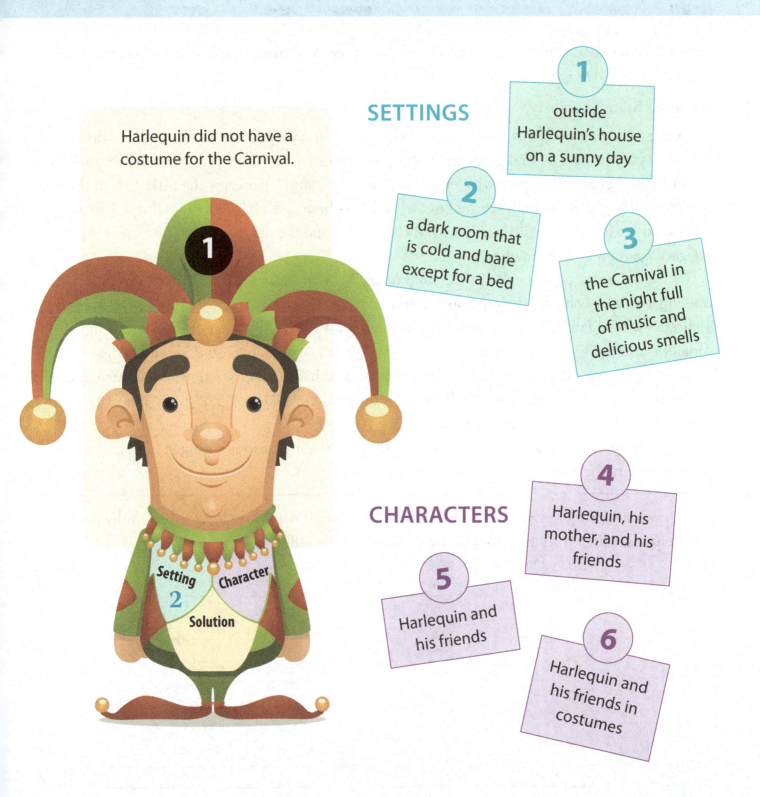

Harlequin did not have a costume for the Carnival.

1

Setting
2
Character

Solution

SETTINGS

1 outside Harlequin's house on a sunny day

2 a dark room that is cold and bare except for a bed

3 the Carnival in the night full of music and delicious smells

CHARACTERS

4 Harlequin, his mother, and his friends

5 Harlequin and his friends

6 Harlequin and his friends in costumes

Name

The bits and scraps that the children gave Harlequin looked like a bunch of rags.

2

The children could not find Harlequin at the Carnival.

3

Setting   Character

Solution

9

Setting   Character

6

Solution

SOLUTIONS

7
The children decide to give Harlequin a bit of each of their costumes.

8
The friends recognize the pieces of their own costumes that are now part of Harlequin's costume.

9
Harlequin's mother sews the patches onto his suit to make a colorful costume.

captives	awkwardly
dismounted	uselessness
gnarled	addressed
disguise	rigid

Fill in the blanks.

1. Andrew, a Confederate soldier in the Civil War, had been captured by the Union Army of the North. He was extremely discouraged by the _____ (*not serving any purpose*) of the struggle.

2. The _____ (*people that are captured*), Andrew and a group of other Confederate soldiers, had gathered secretly.

3. Their leader, Nate, had _____ (*spoken to*) them, trying to raise their spirits.

4. Nate had a plan for escape. When the enemy officer _____ (*got off his horse*), two of the captives would jump on him and tie him up.

5. Because the Union officer was always stiff and _____ (*stiff*), looking neither to the left nor the right, it would be easy to surprise him.

6. The prisoners would tie the officer to the old, _____ (*bent and twisted*) tree that was in the farthest corner of the prison camp.

7. Then, Nate would take the officer's uniform and _____ (*hide the way something really looks*) himself as a Union officer.

8. It would be easy to mimic the officer's speech, because this officer was shy and always spoke _____ (*uneasily*). Nate would tell the Union soldiers that he needed to take these captives with him, to help him chop down trees in the forest. Once in the forest, they would all escape. Andrew began to feel hopeful.

Name _____

Where Would You Find …?

Circle the correct answer.

1. Where would you find a good **disguise**?

   a. In a library   b. In a costume store

   _____

2. Where would you find an animal that moved **awkwardly**?

   a. Among some tottering newborn lambs   b. Among some graceful racehorses

   _____

3. Where would you find people who have been **addressed**?

   a. At a speech   b. In the post office

   _____

4. Where would you find **captives**?

   a. In a prison camp   b. In a pharmacy

   _____

5. Where would you find someone **dismounting**?

   a. At the top of a mountain   b. At a horse-riding school

   _____

6. Where would you find something **useless**?

   a. In a trash can   b. In a supermarket

   _____

7. Where would you find something **rigid**?

   a. Among different flavors of jello   b. Among steel beams

   _____

8. Where would you find a **gnarled** tree?

   a. In a group of newly planted apple trees   b. In a group of very old oak trees

Write a Story

COURAGE

Claw Foot's dream was to earn a new name by performing an act of courage. His act of courage was finding food for his tribe. You have probably heard many stories of people who performed courageous acts. Choose one of those stories, and write about it.

_____

_____

_____

_____

_____

_____

_____

_____

_____

_____

_____

_____

_____

_____

Character Traits

A writer will not usually name the **character traits** of a character in the story. What the writer will do is have the character say, think, or do things that reveal his or her character traits.

What character traits are revealed in the following sentences?

Circle the correct answer.

1. Mrs. Benton handed back the reports, and Julia saw the big A on the front page of hers. She smiled slightly, and then craned her neck to see what grade Andrea had gotten. Julia had worked very hard to get a better grade than Andrea did on this report. When she saw the A+ on Andrea's report, she frowned. The happiness she'd felt at getting an A was all gone.

   Julia is:

   a. lazy   b. jealous   c. disrespectful

2. "Come on, come on, it's pouring! Let's get inside before we get soaked!" yelled Charlie.
   "You go on ahead," said Ben. "I'll be there in a minute."
   As Charlie ran up the steps into the farmhouse, Ben ran out to the corral to get the horses. "They'll be scared out here in the thunderstorm," he thought to himself. "I'd better get them into their stalls until the storm is over."

   Ben is:

   a. hot-tempered   b. stubborn   c. responsible

3. "It is hot out there," said Della. "I'm so thirsty, I could drink a gallon of water."
   "Me, too," wailed Mindy. "Water, I need water! Oh … I am sooo thirsty!"
   The girls came inside the cabin and drank and drank and drank. They sank into some chairs.
   "Running up the hill was fun, wasn't it?" said Della.
   "No …" groaned Mindy.
   "Why are you groaning?" asked Della. "Didn't you get enough to drink?"
   "Yes, but I was sooo thirsty …"

   Mindy likes to:

   a. complain   b. exercise   c. relax with friends

When we first encounter Claw Foot and Broken Wing, they seem completely different from one another. As we read further, we see that they are different, but also the same in some ways. A Venn diagram allows you to compare the ways in which two people or things are different and the ways in which they are alike.

Write the correct information on the lines provided.

The left and right hand sections of the diagram show how Claw Foot and Broken Wing are different. The middle section shows how the two are alike.

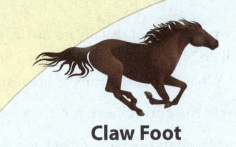

Claw Foot

1. Tribe

2. Approximate age

3. What his tribe needs

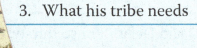

Name _____

Compare and Contrast

Claw Foot and Broken Wing

Broken Wing

1. Their injured limbs

1. Tribe

2. Their names

2. Approximate age

3. What is most important to them

4. The deal they make

3. What he offers to help the Sioux

5. How they feel about one another at the end of the story

sturdy	declared
coarse	lashed
yearned	produce
kindhearted	disbelief

Fill in the blanks.

1. Mimi was a _____ (*strong and not easily hurt*) little dog that had been left behind when her unfeeling owners moved away.

2. She had _____ (*thick and rough*) black hair, big brown eyes, and a tail that never stopped wagging.

3. The one thing she wanted was a _____ (*good and generous*) master to take her in.

4. Sandy was an only child. The one thing she _____ (*wanted very, very much*) for was a little dog to call her own.

5. "If only somehow, some way, I could get a dog, I would be the best friend that dog ever had," she _____ (*said firmly*).

6. As Sandy made her way home, she heard something whimper near the deserted house on her block. What could _____ (*make*) a sound like that? She wondered.

7. She started to look around and saw, _____ (*tied*) to a tree, a sad-looking puppy looking up at her with big, brown eyes.

8. She recognized the dog as having belonged to the people who moved away. She looked at Mimi in _____ (*not believing*). Then she smiled. Her wish had come true.

Using Your Vocabulary Words

You are an author, though you may not know it! Below are the first sentences of seven different stories. Each sentence uses one of your vocabulary words. Write a second sentence that goes with the first, and could be a good beginning for a story. The first one is done for you.

1. The cowboy looked around for a **sturdy** rope.

    He was planning to catch the wild horse he'd seen out on the prairie.
    _____

2. When the sailors saw how strong the wind was, they **lashed** everything on deck to the mast.

    _____

    _____

3. "I will not!" **declared** Jamie, stamping his foot.

    _____

    _____

4. The **kindhearted** storekeeper waited patiently as Jennifer reached into her pocket for her money.

    _____

    _____

5. Our family likes to visit factories that **produce** all kinds of interesting items.

    _____

    _____

6. When Mrs. Kimball reached over to clear the table, Mandy noticed how **coarse** her hands were.

    _____

    _____

7. All his life, Ron had **yearned** to climb the high mountain that was right at the edge of their village.

    _____

Important Reasons

More than anything else, Beatrice wanted to go to school. Does that surprise you? Many children complain about having to go to school. Deep down, though, every child knows how important school is. Write two paragraphs about the reasons that going to school is such an important part of growing up.

_____

_____

_____

_____

_____

_____

_____

_____

_____

_____

_____

_____

_____

_____

_____

Fact/Opinion

Whenever you read or hear something, the first thing you should ask is: Is this fact or opinion? A **fact** is something that is true. An **opinion** is something that cannot be proven, and which may or may not be true.

Next to each of the following statements, write an F for Fact or an O for Opinion.

1. _____ George Washington was the first president of the United States.

2. _____ George Washington was the best president of the United States.

3. _____ Bears hibernate in the winter.

4. _____ Daffodils are some of the first flowers to bloom in the spring.

5. _____ Chocolate is the best flavor of ice cream.

6. _____ "This soup is good, but it is too salty."

7. _____ If you have 20/20 vision you do not need glasses.

8. _____ The best way to travel is by car.

9. _____ Monkeys are the cutest animals in the zoo.

10. _____ World War II started in the year 1939.

11. _____ There are more daylight hours in the summer than there are in the winter.

12. _____ The best way to spend your summer is to go to sleepaway camp.

13. _____ The lunch they serve in school on Wednesday is the best one of the week.

14. _____ Panda bears feed mainly on bamboo.

BEATRICE'S GOAT
Graphic Organizer

Beatrice would probably divide her childhood into before Mugisa came and after Mugisa came. That is because, in so many ways, Beatrice's life changed with the coming of Mugisa. In this exercise, each question has two answers: one for "before Mugisa" and one for "after Mugisa." Select the correct answer from the lists at the bottom of each page and write the numbers of the correct answers into the milk bottles.

1. How did Beatrice spend her day before Mugisa?
Before **3**   After **4**

2. Did Beatrice think she would ever be able to go to school?
Before   After

3. Did Beatrice think owning a goat could help her family?
Before   After

4. How many goats did Beatrice think the family was getting?
Before   After

Before Mugisa

1. No. Beatrice could not imagine how a goat could be of help.
2. Beatrice thought they were getting one goat.
3. Beatrice helped Mama in the fields, tended the chickens, and watched the children.
4. No, she thought she would never be able to pay for books or a uniform.

After Mugisa

1. Yes, she felt she would one day be able to go to school.
2. Two weeks after Mugisa arrived she gave birth to twins, so the family now owned three goats.
3. Beatrice learned that a goat could provide milk that could be sold.
4. Beatrice spent her day taking care of Mugisa and her two kids.

Before and After

1. Had Beatrice ever tasted goat's milk?

Before   After

2. How did the family make extra money?

Before   After

3. Did the children have the clothes and blankets they needed?

 Before    After

4. What would Beatrice say to Bunane when he said he wanted to go to school?

Before   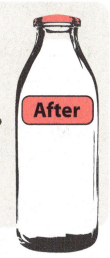 After

Before Mugisa

1. She would not have had anything reassuring to say.
2. There was no way they could earn extra money.
3. No, they did not have everything they needed.
4. No, she didn't even know what it tasted like.

After Mugisa

1. Selling Mugisa's milk brought in a lot of extra money.
2. Yes, and she loved its sweet taste.
3. Now Mama could buy some of the things they needed.
4. She could encourage him by telling him that his family would soon own a goat, too.

corresponded	nurtured
efficiently	sprouting
employed	survive
gravely	vessels

Fill in the blanks.

1. Miss Weatherbottom was a secretary in the law offices of the Woodward brothers. She typed
    _____ (*in the most practical way*), filed _____
    (*in the most practical way*), and even ate _____ (*in the most
    practical way*).

2. When she spoke, she spoke slowly and _____ (*seriously*).

3. The plants on her windowsill seemed to be _____ (*beginning to
    grow*) almost as soon as she planted the seeds.

4. This was because she _____ (*supported and encouraged*) them,
    watered them, fed them plant food, and commanded them to grow.

5. Miss Weatherbottom did not serve coffee in cups or mugs; she served it in
    "_____" (*a formal word for cup, bowl, or pitcher*).

6. Mr. James Woodward, who _____ (*hired to do a job*) her, was a
    fun-loving young man.

7. Although he was glad Miss Weatherbottom was so efficient, he sometimes thought he would
    not _____ (*live through*) one of her long speeches on how to be
    more efficient.

8. After a while, he gave up trying to get a word in edgewise, and just _____
    (*wrote letters*) with her, writing her letters to tell her what he wanted.

Who? What? Where? When? How?

Circle the correct answer.

1. *Who* speaks more **gravely**?

   a. A person with bad news

   b. A comedian

2. *What* helps a seedling **sprout**?

   a. A lack of rain

   b. Careful watering

3. *Where* would you find a **vessel**?

   a. In a kitchen cabinet

   b. In a garden

4. *When* would you **employ** some extra help?

   a. When you had very little work that needed doing

   b. When you had a lot of work that had to be done

5. *What* kinds of animals will **survive** a flash flood?

   a. Animals who cannot swim

   b. Animals who can swim

6. *How* would you **nurture** a young, weak plant?

   a. You would water it and tie a stake to it

   b. You would pull it out by its roots

7. *Who* probably types more **efficiently**?

   a. A secretary

   b. A monkey

8. *What* do you use to **correspond** with someone?

   a. A cell phone

   b. A pen and paper

Write a Diary Entry

DEAR
DIARY

In *The Gardener,* Uncle Jim is so quiet that we never really know what he is thinking. But if you understand the character of Uncle Jim, you probably have a good idea of what his thoughts were. Pretend that Uncle Jim kept a diary. Write two entries in the diary that tell us what he was thinking on those days. The first entry should be for the day Lydia Grace arrived. The second entry should be for the day of "the big surprise" on the roof.

_____

_____

_____

_____

_____

_____

_____

_____

_____

_____

_____

_____

_____

_____

Compare and Contrast

Much of our thinking is comparing and contrasting. When you **compare** things, you show how they are alike. When you **contrast** things, you show how they are different.

The two kittens were adorable. They were about two months old and loved playing hide and seek with each other. One was ginger-colored and the other was jet black. Although both of them had green eyes, the eyes of the black kitten seemed to glow like jewels, while the eyes of the ginger cat just looked friendly and warm.

Give two ways in which the kittens are similar.

1. _____

2. _____

Give two ways in which the kittens are different.

1. _____

2. _____

You would think twins would be alike, but these twins were hardly alike at all! First of all, Jen was a girl and Ben was a boy. Jen had red hair and Ben had blond hair. Jen loved books and clothes. Ben loved trucks and balls. But they were alike in some ways. They both hated to go to bed on time. They were both sleepy in the morning. They both liked apples and chocolate and hated soft-boiled eggs. They were alike in one more way—they had the same birthday!

In what three ways are Jen and Ben different?

1. _____

2. _____

3. _____

In what three ways are Jen and Ben alike?

1. _____

2. _____

3. _____

Lydia Grace was a gardener in more ways than one. She planted bulbs that grew into flowers, but she also "planted" good deeds. Those deeds produced beautiful "flowers," too! In the pictures below, each bulb represents a good deed and its flower represents its result. In every picture, either the flower or the bulb has been left blank. Complete the pictures by filling in the blanks. Choose your answers from the answer box and write its number into the flower or the bulb.

The seeds flowered into a beautiful garden.

3.

4

1.
Lydia Grace wrote a long poem for Uncle Jim.

2.
Lydia Grace taught Emma Latin.

4.
Lydia Grace worked hard to keep her surprise a secret.

1. Emma taught Lydia Grace how to knead bread.

2. Uncle Jim was very, very surprised and happy at the end.

3. Lydia Grace planted all the seeds that Grandma sent.

4. Uncle Jim put it in his pocket, showing that it meant a lot to him.

Name

Cause and Effect

The neighbors and customers gave Lydia Grace gifts of plants.

Lydia Grace had a wonderful year instead of a miserable one.

6.

8.

5.

7.

Lydia Grace was very nice and helpful to Emma.

Lydia Grace cared about Uncle Jim and wanted him to be happy.

5. Lydia Grace planted flowers and vegetables where others could enjoy them.

6. Uncle Jim showed Lydia Grace how much he loved her by baking her a beautiful cake.

7. Lydia Grace was cheerful and friendly throughout the year.

8. Emma helped Lydia Grace with her secret garden.

quarries	confidence
garnet	hesitation
mineralogist	solemnly
admiration	lift

Fill in the blanks.

1. I had been around mines and _____ (*pits that contain large amounts of stones*) all my life.

2. That's because my father is an expert on all kinds of precious and semiprecious stones. He is a _____ (*a scientist who studies minerals*).

3. My father's favorite stone is the _____ (*a deep red stone*), which is usually a deep red.

4. However, we had come to Africa to look for the rare blue garnet. Our search had been held up when our car broke down. After putting it on the _____ (*a device that lifts cars so the mechanic can repair them*), the mechanic was able to fix it quickly.

5. Although no one had found a blue garnet right in this area, my father had _____ (*belief in oneself and one's ideas*) that there were some here.

6. The African guide had _____ (*seriously*) said, "No one has ever found a blue garnet in this entire area. You must go south to find the famed blue garnet."

7. My father answered without _____ (*a brief pause*), " I know from my research that aside from many red garnets, there are also some blue garnets to be found here."

8. We searched and dug for three days. We found garnets of many colors, but not one blue one. Finally, we heard a cry from my father. "I found it! A whole group of deep blue garnets!" I ran to my father and we looked at the beautiful, twinkling stones in _____ (*a feeling of respect*).

Word Play

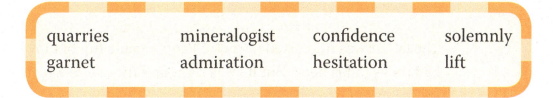

| quarries | mineralogist | confidence | solemnly |
| garnet | admiration | hesitation | lift |

Choose the correct word from the word box above.

1. What is a one-syllable word that gives your car a fun ride? _____

2. What is a two-syllable word that rhymes with stories? _____

3. What is a two-syllable word that includes something that fishermen use? _____

4. What is a three-syllable word that has a silent letter in it? _____

5. What is a three-syllable word whose last syllable sounds like something you do not want in your car? _____

6. What is a four-syllable word that has some sunshine in it? _____

7. What is a four-syllable word that has a word in it that is the opposite of "stand"? _____

8. What is a five-syllable word that has a word in it that means "rocks"? _____

Ideas

VALUABLE

I
D
E
A
S

The father was interested in rocks. People made fun of him, saying he had rocks in his head. But he was right and they were wrong. The study of rocks is not a waste of time. It is not unusual for people to laugh at ideas of value. Write about an inventor whose idea was ridiculed. Or, you may write about any new idea that was thought useless or ridiculous at first. If you don't know any true stories, you may make one up.

Generalizing

When we **generalize**, we make a general statement based on a number of facts. For example, if we read that some dogs watch sheep, some dogs guide vision-impaired people, and some dogs are used to locate items that are lost, we can *generalize* and say that dogs are helpful to people.

Make a generalization based on the group of facts in the following paragraphs.

1. Maxy sat on the ground and wailed. He'd been riding his new tricycle and hit a bump in the sidewalk. The tricycle had turned over and dumped Maxy on the cement. Melissa was the first to reach him. "What's wrong, Maxy? Does anything hurt?" Before Maxy could answer, Harold ran over to Maxy and stood the tricycle back up. "Don't worry, Maxy, your tricycle didn't get scratched. Wow, but it's shiny. Are you okay?" Pete hurried over and said, "Hey, Maxy. I saw you fall. Are you bleeding? Should I call your brother?" Maxy smiled and stood up. "I'm alright," he said, and climbed back onto his tricycle.

   What generalization could you make about the kids on Maxy's block?

   _____

   _____

   _____

   _____

2. Let me tell you about my cousins. There are four boys in the family: Phil, who is sixteen, Don, who is fourteen, Barry, who is eleven, and Jacob, who is seven. Phil plays the clarinet, Don plays the saxophone, Barry plays the drums, and Jacob plays the piano. Phil is great at basketball but hates football, Don likes ice hockey, Barry won't play anything but baseball, and Jacob is a soccer guy.

   What two generalizations could you make about the cousins?

   _____

   _____

   _____

The father's life was full of interesting twists and turns. He had many different jobs and met many interesting people. But one thing never changed: his love of rocks. At the end of the story, the father's lifelong dream comes true. He is able to devote his entire day to the study of rocks—and be paid for it, too!

Each picture on these two pages represents one step in the father's life, leading up to the position of curator at the museum.

Put the pictures in their proper order by numbering them. Write your answer on the rock.

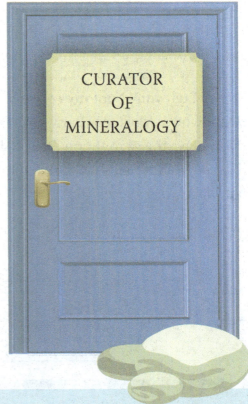

CURATOR
OF
MINERALOGY

Name _____

Sequencing

considered   inhabitants
reassuring   unaccustomed
temptingly   withdrawn
delicacy   vanished

Fill in the blanks.

1. Richard and Rachel stood at the door of the palace, their eyes opened wide. It was built in a

   magnificent, _____ (*unusual*) style.

2. Every year, the king and queen invited two children from the village to tour the palace and

   join the royal family for tea. Every kind of _____ (*delicious food*)

   was served at that time.

3. The servant opened the door for the children, showed them into a large room, and then

   _____ (*disappeared*).

4. Richard and Rachel were a little frightened to be alone in the huge palace. They wondered

   where the other _____ (*people who live there*) of the palace were.

5. Two maids had come in, taken their coats, and shown them some chairs. They had then

   _____ (*left*).

6. Just as they began _____ (*giving confidence to*) one another, another

   maid came in.

7. The maid placed some cream puffs and hot chocolate _____ (*in a

   way that makes one want it*) on the table.

8. "Would you like to eat a little something before the tour?" she asked the children. Richard

   and Rachel _____ (*thought about something*) for a moment. "Will

   there still be tea afterwards?" Rachel asked. "Of course," said the maid. "We always have tea,

   no matter what." "In that case," said Richard, "we'd love to have a little snack." And, in a flash,

   the cream puffs and cocoa vanished!

If ...

Circle the correct answer.

1. If you were served **delicacies**, would you

    a. eat them slowly with a smile **or** b. swallow them down like medicine?

    _____

2. If you were **unaccustomed** to taking long walks, would you

    a. be short of breath after half an hour **or** b. easily walk for an hour?

    _____

3. If your wallet had **vanished**, would you be

    a. glad there was so much money in it **or** b. worried there was so much money in it?

    _____

4. If you have **considered** a problem, have you

    a. thought carefully about it **or** b. hardly thought about it at all?

    _____

5. If your friend is the kind who is **reassuring**, would it be better to

    a. talk to her when you are worried **or** b. avoid talking to her when you are worried?

    _____

6. If your pet turtle's head is **withdrawn**, can you

    a. see its friendly face **or** b. see only its shell?

    _____

7. If a city has no **inhabitants**, is it

    a. a ghost town **or** b. a very crowded city?

    _____

8. If you find chocolate ice cream **tempting**, do you

    a. love chocolate ice cream **or** b. dislike chocolate ice cream?

What Does an Animal Think?

We often talk about pets or other animals. Do you ever wonder what the animals are thinking about *you*? Choose an animal. It could be your or someone else's pet. It could be a stray animal that you feed. It could be an animal in the zoo. Write two paragraphs. In the first paragraph, write some thoughts you have about this animal. In the second paragraph, write some thoughts this animal has about you!

A
N
I
M
A
L
S

_____

_____

_____

_____

_____

_____

_____

_____

_____

_____

_____

_____

_____

_____

_____

Name _____

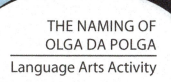
Fantasy and Reality

Sometimes little children have trouble knowing the difference between fantasy and reality. As we grow older, we learn to easily tell the difference. **Fantasy** is something that is not only made up, it is something that could *never* happen, like a person growing wings and flying. **Reality** may be true or made up, but it is something that *could* happen.

Next to each of the following sentences, write an F for fantasy or an R for reality.

1. _____ "I'm late," said the White Rabbit as he scurried towards the rabbit hole.

   _____

2. _____ Exhausted, the miner put down his shovel and sat on the ground. He did not know when help would come; he just knew he could no longer try to dig his way out of the mine.

   _____

3. _____ The children looked up in amazement. The owl, high in the tree, winked at them and said, "Wait here. I'm going to bring you some wings, and when you've put them on, we'll fly to my nest together."

   _____

4. _____ Young Joseph ran after the goat as it entered a tunnel. He ran and ran. It seemed forever before he saw a light. When he finally came out of the tunnel, he saw a palace made of emeralds and rubies shining in the sun. The streets were paved with gold, and diamonds hung from the trees. "What place is this?" he wondered.

   _____

5. _____ The wagon train wound its way slowly over the mountain. They hadn't seen a town, or even an outpost, for two weeks. "Where are we?" wondered Jethro, as he trudged next to his family's covered wagon. Would they ever get to California? He doubted it.

In the following exercise, we have divided *The Naming of Olga da Polga* into four sections. For two of the sections, we have named the section. It is your job to summarize what is in that section of the story. For two of the sections, we have summarized the story. It is your job to name the section.

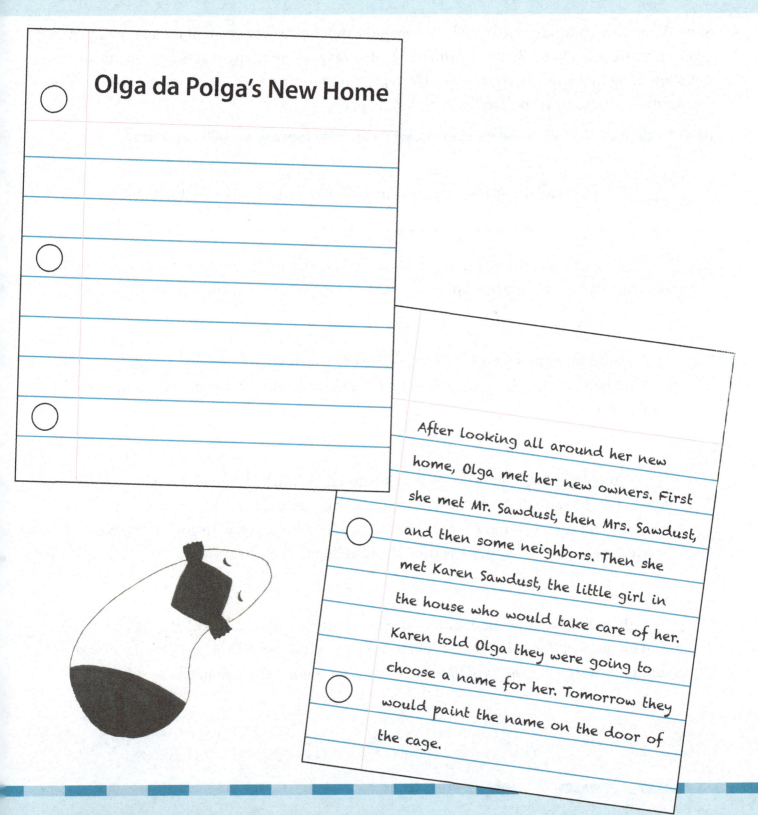

Olga da Polga's New Home

○

○

○

After looking all around her new home, Olga met her new owners. First she met Mr. Sawdust, then Mrs. Sawdust, and then some neighbors. Then she met Karen Sawdust, the little girl in the house who would take care of her. Karen told Olga they were going to choose a name for her. Tomorrow they would paint the name on the door of the cage.

Olga Decides She Must Tell Karen Her Name

○

○

○

○ Finally Olga had finished writing her name in the sawdust. She went to bed. When Karen saw the name, she could read it. She called her mother, but her

○ mother couldn't see anything in the sawdust. Still, Karen's mother liked the name, and Karen and Olga were very happy with a sign that would say

○ "Olga da Polga."

> cautiously   gratitude
> countless   snooze
> dazzled   sputtering
> glistening   sturdy

Fill in the blanks.

1. Franklin loved toy trains. His mother had set up a big, _____ (*strong and solid*) table in the basement for his train set.

2. He had covered the table with tracks, artificial trees, miniature houses, and _____ (*very many*) train signals.

3. It was the night before Franklin's birthday, and he was too excited to fall asleep. He knew that sometime in the night, his parents would put on the table the shiny, _____ (*shining*) red engine that he'd wanted for a very long time.

4. Franklin decided he would surprise them by being right there in the basement when they brought down his engine, and would express his _____ (*appreciation*) by holding up a big sign that said "Thank You!"

5. At 10:00, clutching his sign, Franklin _____ (*carefully*) tiptoed down the stairs and hid in a shadowy corner of the basement, so his parents wouldn't notice him.

6. At 10:30, his eyes were closing, and he took a short _____ (*nap*).

7. At 11:00, he was awakened by the sound of an engine _____ (*making popping sounds*).

8. Opening his eyes, he saw his father trying to start the shiny red engine. With a rumble, the engine took off and started speeding around the tracks. Franklin was _____ (*overpowered by brightness*)! Forgetting all about his sign and his surprise thank you, he jumped up and hugged his parents.

Opposites

This exercise is a little tricky! You must read each sentence, and then choose the vocabulary word that is the *opposite* of the words in italics. Good luck!

Circle the correct answer.

1. Jack turned on the ignition, and the car started up immediately. The motor *purred like a kitten*.

    cautiously   (sputtered)   sturdy

2. The boy, frightened by the barking of the huge dog, *carelessly* ran into the street without looking to see if any cars were coming.

    countless   snooze   cautiously

3. It was a winter afternoon, and the *light was so dull* that Virginia could hardly see more than a few yards in front of her.

    dazzling   sturdy   countless

4. Mr. Dinkins was furious. What *a lack of appreciation* that fellow had, he fumed.

    glistened   gratitude   countless

5. Sarah woke up refreshed and energetic. She'd had *a long, deep sleep*.

    dazzled   cautiously   snooze

6. Henry looked up at the winter sky. *Only a few* stars were out; most were covered by clouds.

    countless   sputtered   snooze

7. Yesterday, the snow was white and new, sparkling in the sun. Today, it was gray and matted; *it was dull* and depressing.

    glistened   sturdy   gratitude

Write a Story

A Toad for Tuesday starts out like this:

> *On a windy, wintry night, as countless stars were shining bright,
> deep in the ground, far under the snow,*

Using this as a first line, continue writing a new and different story.
You don't need to finish the story, just write two paragraphs of a tale
that sounds like it will be worth reading!

Name _____

Reviewing Story Elements

It is time to review the elements that make up a story: plot, character, setting, and main idea. Which element does each of the following sentences describe?

Put a check mark next to the correct answer.

1. Admiral Brighton was tall, muscular, and not afraid of anyone or anything. His dark eyes never softened, and his lips never smiled.

   _____ Plot _____ Character _____ Setting _____ Main Idea

2. The sea air was salty, as they sailed over the endless blue water under the endless blue sky. There was not another ship in the water, and there was not a cloud in the sky.

   _____ Plot _____ Character _____ Setting _____ Main Idea

3. Jonas climbed the rigging and looked over the water through his spyglass. He could see a small boat way in the distance. It was a pirate ship, and it was headed in his direction.

   _____ Plot _____ Character _____ Setting _____ Main Idea

4. Below deck, Ned, the cook, bustled around. He was fat, jolly, and red-cheeked.

   _____ Plot _____ Character _____ Setting _____ Main Idea

5. Jonas ran to tell the admiral about the pirate ship. The admiral just looked at him and said, "We will not run from anyone. We will stand our ground and fight. Fear is the worst feeling a person can have."

   _____ Plot _____ Character _____ Setting _____ Main Idea

A TOAD FOR TUESDAY
PART ONE
Graphic Organizer

Warton and Morton lived in a warm, cozy home. It takes some work to make a home warm and cozy, and Warton and Morton divided the work up. Do you know how? (Look back at the story to double-check.) In the picture below, we have pointed out how clean the house was and how good the food was. We have also pointed out some character traits, because those create the home's atmosphere. In each box, circle the name of the toad who did the work or had the personality trait described.

Eyes that blink when he thinks

WARTON

MORTON

He brings a calm good nature into the home

WARTON

MORTON

A clean, polished table

WARTON

MORTON

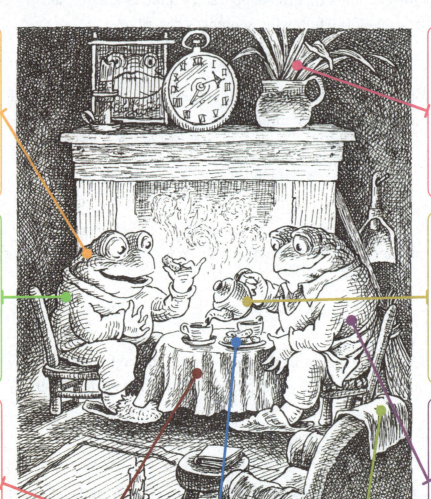

A well-cared-for plant

WARTON

MORTON

Delicious clover blossom tea

WARTON

MORTON

He is very helpful

WARTON

MORTON

A laundered tablecloth

WARTON

MORTON

Fine beetle brittle

WARTON

MORTON

An antimacassar on the chair to keep it clean

WARTON

MORTON

Graphic Organizer

Name

When Warton left home, he was wearing many clothes to keep him warm. He also had a knapsack full of extras for the trip. Draw a line from each picture to either the knapsack where it was packed or to the place on Warton's body where it was worn.

Some lunches

2 pairs of mittens

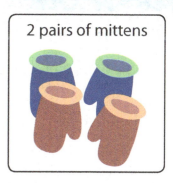

3 sweaters

4 coats

Furry slippers

Skis

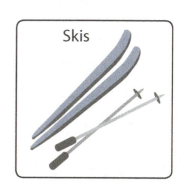

Warm cap

Beetle brittle

An extra pair of mittens

dreary	astonished
flustered	unravel
flabbergasted	snarled
refreshing	talons

Fill in the blanks.

1. She looked like a fussy old lady, confused and _____ (*nervous*).

2. I thought our visit was just to brighten up her _____ (*gloomy*) life.

3. When my friend and I walked through the door of the house I was _____ (*very surprised*) to see several cages with pigeons in them lined up in her front room.

4. My friend's aunt invited us into her small kitchen and gave us a cool drink that was surprisingly _____ (*something that renews your energy*).

5. As we sat there, she picked up a piece of knitting and looked at it closely. She took out a book and wrote something in it. Then she began to _____ (*take apart threads*) the knitting.

6. The next thing I knew, her cat dropped the _____ (*tangled*) yarn and ran to the door. When Martin's old aunt opened the door, an enemy soldier was standing there. Seeing a little old lady, he said, "They told me a dangerous spy lived here, but, I see only an old woman."

7. A moment later, there was a scratching at the window. A pigeon was right outside, holding a piece of knitting in his _____ (*claws*).

8. The old woman let the pigeon in, took the piece of knitting out of its talons, looked at it closely, wrote something in her book, and unraveled the knitting. I was _____ (*completely surprised*). "My little old aunt is a spy. The knitting has a secret code in it, which she reads, writes down, and then unravels. Then she sends the pigeons back for more messages." "Wow!" I thought. What a spy! What an aunt!

Putting Your Vocabulary to Work

In the following exercise, circle the phrase in which the word is used properly.

1. **dreary**

   a. It was a dark and dreary day.

   b. The hamburger was dry and dreary.

2. **flustered**

   a. The woman stood at the window looking lonely and flustered in the silent house.

   b. When the boss walked in, the secretary got flustered and dropped a whole batch of important papers.

3. **flabbergasted**

   a. When Farmer Joe entered the barn and saw his cow Flossie calmly chewing straw, he was flabbergasted. Why just yesterday, she'd been terribly sick!

   b. Jimmy sat in class, listening as the teacher reviewed the lesson. He'd understood it the first time, and having to hear it again left him feeling flabbergasted.

4. **refreshing**

   a. Sandy took a long, thirsty sip of ice cold lemonade. "Nothing in this world," she thought, "is as refreshing as lemonade on a hot day."

   b. Bernie huddled under his covers, feeling chilled and feverish all at the same time. He sipped at some lukewarm, refreshing tea, which was all he could swallow.

5. **astonished**

   a. "I am astonished to see you here," said the principal to Donnie, when he met him at the store in the middle of a school day.

   b. "I am astonished to see you here," said the librarian to Sally when she walked into the library, as she always did, on Wednesday afternoon right after school.

The Best Way

In the many stories you have read this year, characters have traveled in a variety of ways. Some sailed in ships. Some drove in automobiles. Some bumped along in carts or wagons. One took a train. Another flew in a plane, while others rode on horseback. Warton was flown over the treetops by George! What is *your* favorite way to travel? Write two paragraphs describing what you think is the best way to travel and why it is better than the other ways.

_____

_____

_____

_____

_____

_____

_____

_____

_____

_____

_____

_____

_____

TRAVELER

Characters' Actions

rushed	humid	silvery	brightly	frightened	slimy	meanest
creaky	snowing	rattle	grouchy	clean	tall	

Words are the tools we use to describe people, objects, thoughts, and feelings.
Choose a word from the word bank to complete the sentences.

1. The air was hot and _____. Gramps and Gram sat on their front
    porch and fanned themselves as they rocked back and forth in their _____,
    squeaky rocking chairs.

2. The alligator slithered through the thick, _____ mud. He was the
    longest, ugliest, and _____ looking alligator I'd ever seen.

3. Pop, pop, pop went the popcorn. Little Jessica had taken the lid off of the popcorn maker, and
    popcorn was _____ down all over Mom's spotlessly
    _____ kitchen floor like flakes of pure white snow.

4. Silently the Indian scout walked through the dark woods. He found his way by the light of
    the gleaming _____ moon that shone _____
    through the leaves.

5. Mr. Clark, who owned the candy store, was a _____, short-
    tempered man. The kids were a little afraid of him and asked for candy in soft,
    _____ voices.

6. New York City is full of _____ buildings. The people hurry along
    the streets, always looking busy and _____. The horns toot loudly,
    and the subways _____ and roar beneath the ground.

A TOAD FOR TUESDAY
PART TWO

Graphic Organizer

In this section of the story, the owl, George, changes for the better, thanks to Warton's good influence. The chart below is divided into two. On the left hand side, there are sentences that describe George before he met Warton. In the column on the right hand side, write down how George changed for the better after he met Warton.

The owl's home is dirty and messy.	The nest is now neat and clean.
The owl doesn't have a name.	
The owl doesn't have a friend.	
George says he doesn't want any tea.	
George has never laughed.	
George never said "goodnight" to anyone.	
George usually stayed out very late.	
George had no one to tell his troubles to.	

Name

Draw a line from each problem in the boxes to the picture that shows how Warton dealt with that problem.

The nest was dark and dreary the first night.

Warton was cold and uncomfortable the first night.

Warton was cold and tired and needed something hot and refreshing.

The nest was a mess.

Warton missed good conversation.

The owl's nest was so high that there was no way to escape from it.

George kept reminding Warton that he would eat him.

Hope

While George, the owl, changed for the better from day to day, Warton, the toad, was living under the threat of death. Yet, he remained cheerful and friendly. He cheered himself up by doing things and by hoping for the best. How did Warton deal with the following problems during the five days he was George's prisoner?

bewilderment	passageway
exasperated	stirring
gaped	tattered
immensely	wooded

Fill in the blanks.

1. It was midnight and somebody was pounding on the door. I opened the door wide and
   _____ (*opened my mouth and stared*).

2. Standing there was young Jed, his clothing dirty and _____
   (*torn and ragged*).

3. The sight of this strong, young man looking so crushed was _____
   (*arousing one's emotions*).

4. "What was he doing here?" I thought in _____ (*confusion*).

5. Only yesterday he'd told my father that he was leaving our farm to go and seek his fortune.
   My father was _____ (*fed up*) with him and his dreams, but wished
   him farewell.

6. Now, he had returned to our farm, the only farm around for miles in the lonely,
   _____ (*having many trees*) area.

7. Jed stood in the _____ (*a hall*), seemingly unable to move.

8. He looked _____ (*very, very*) tired. He took two steps forward and
   dropped in exhaustion. Where had he been?

Name One Thing That …

In this activity, you will have to tell a little about yourself. Make sure you know what the word means before you write your answer.

1. Name one thing that causes you **bewilderment**.

   _____

   _____

2. Name one thing that makes you **exasperated**.

   _____

   _____

3. Name one thing that would make you **gape**.

   _____

   _____

4. Name one thing that you love **immensely**.

   _____

   _____

5. Name one place where you have seen a **passageway**.

   _____

   _____

6. Name one thing that requires a lot of **stirring**.

   _____

   _____

7. Name one thing you own that is **tattered**.

   _____

   _____

8. Name one place you know of that is **wooded**.

   _____

Write a Thank You Note

When Warton arrived at Aunt Toolia's, he told her the entire story of what had happened to him on his way to her house. After he went home, Aunt Toolia sat down to write him a note thanking him for the delicious beetle brittle. She also wanted to tell him how much she admired what he had done for George, the owl. Write a beautiful thank you note that expresses Aunt Toolia's feelings. If you have time, you may decorate it.

_____

_____

_____

_____

_____

_____

_____

_____

_____

_____

_____

_____

_____

_____

Name _____

Illustration

Most readers love good illustrations. The writer loves illustrations, too, because they help tell the reader about the story's setting and characters.

The *setting* of a story is when and where a story takes place. But there is more. The setting creates the *mood* of the story, too. The story's mood may be happy or frightening or comical. Look at the illustration on this page.

> What mood does it create for the story?
> **Circle one answer.**
>
> scary   mysterious
>
> funny   cozy   happy

What in the picture tells us that it's cold outside? _____

What in the picture tells us what the time of day is? _____

The illustration tells us about the characters, too. In this picture, the character on the left is Warton, and the character on the right is Morton.

1. How do you know that Warton is good-natured? _____

2. How do you know that Morton enjoys serving meals? _____

3. Most important, what feeling is there between the brothers? What in the picture makes you feel that way? _____

WHOOO ...?

... came to rescue Warton? _____

... did Warton think would miss him the most if the owl ate him? _____

... did Warton see in the distance as he and the mice skied over the snow? _____

... was attacking George? _____

... had told George how good juniper-berry tea was? _____

... did George really want as a friend? _____

... did Warton really want as a friend? _____

... gave Warton a ride to Aunt Toolia's? _____

... probably enjoyed the beetle brittle to the very last drop?
_____

Name

Find the answers to the owl's questions by searching through the mice's answers on this page. Write the answers on the line next to the question.

A fox

Warton

Warton

George

George

George

Morton

Aunt Toolia

Sy

Glossary

A

addressed (uh DRESSD) *v.*: directed his words to

admiration (AD mih RAY shun) *n.*: respect and approval

ambition (am BIH shun) *n.*: a goal that someone has

astonished (uh STAHN isht) *adj.*: extremely surprised

awkwardly (AWK wurd lee) *adv.*: uneasily; uncomfortably

B

befitting (bih FIT ing) *adj.*: proper for; fitting

bewilderment (bih WIL dur ment) *n.*: confusion

briefly (BREEF lee) *adv.*: for a short time

bruised (BROOZED) *adj.*: slightly injured

burrowed (BURR ode) *v.*: living in a hole dug deep in the ground

C

captives (KAP tivs) *n.*: people that are captured

carousel (KER uh SEL) *n.*: a merry-go-round

cautiously (KAW shus lee) *adv.*: carefully and a bit anxiously

chaos (KAY ahss) *n.*: complete confusion

circumference (sur KUM fer unts) *n.*: the border of a circle

clattered (KLATT erd) *v.*: made a loud, rattling sound

coarse (KORSE) *adj.*: thick and rough

cobblestones (KAH bl STONES) *n.*: a naturally rounded stone that was used to pave streets

cocoon (kuh KOON) *n.*: a silky case in which certain insects enclose their eggs

confessed (kun FEST) *v.*: admitted to a wrongdoing

confidence (KAHN fih DENTS) *n.*: belief in oneself

considered (kun SID erd) *adj.*: thought about

constant (KAHN stunt) *adj.*: continuing without a stop

converge (kuhn VURJ) *v.*: meet

correspond (KOR ih SPOND) *v.*: to exchange letters with someone

countless (KOWNT less) *adj.*: a large number of something; too many to count

coward (KOW urd) *n.*: one who is fearful and lacks courage

craving (KRAY ving) *n.*: a strong desire for something

Glossary

crouched (KROWCHD) *v.*: stooped low to the ground

cyclone (SIKE lone) *n.*: a very strong storm in which the wind blows in a great circle

D

darted (DART ed) *v.*: started suddenly and ran swiftly

dazzled (DAZ uld) *v.*: overpowered by the brightness of something

debated (dih BAYT ed) *v.*: argued

declared (dih KLAIRD) *v.*: said firmly

define (dee FINE) *v.*: explain

delicacies (DEL ih kuh seez) *n.*: delicious food

descends (dih SENDS) *v.*: comes down

desperate (DESS prut) *adj.*: done because of tremendous need

determination (dee TUR mih NAY shun) *n.*: the strong will to do something

disbelief (DIS bih LEEF) *n.*: not believing

disguise (dis GIZE) *v.*: to hide the way something looks

dismount (DIS mount) *v.*: to get off a horse

dodged (DOJD) *v.*: avoided by jumping aside

dreary (DREER ee) *adj.*: gloomy and sad

drought (DROWT) *n.*: a lack of rain

E

efficiently (e FISH int lee) *adv.*: doing something in the best, most practical way

employed (em PLOYD) *v.*: hired to do a job

enable (en AY bul) *v.*: make possible

enormous (ih NORR muss) *adj.*: huge

etched (ETCHD) *v.*: sharply outlined

exasperated (ig ZASS per AYT ed) *adj.*: fed up; very annoyed

F

fatal (FAY tul) *adj.*: something that causes death

fertile (FUR tuhl) *adj.*: the type of soil or land in which plants grow easily

fierce (FEERSS) *adj.*: extremely strong and wild

flabbergasted (FLAB er GASS ted) *adj.*: completely surprised

flexible (FLEX ih bul) *adj.*: willing and able to make changes

flickered (FLIK erd) *v.*: shone with a wavering light

flustered (FLUSS terd) *adj.*: nervous and confused

frail (FRAYL) *adj.*: weak and easily injured

Glossary

fringe (FRINJ) *v.*: to make a fringe, a border of loose threads at the end of a scarf or shawl

G

gaped (GAIPT) *v.*: stared at in wonder with an open mouth

garnets (GAR nets) *n.*: a semiprecious stone that is a deep red color

gawk (GAWK) *v.*: stare

glistened (GLISS und) *v.*: shone and sparkled

gnarled (NARLD) *adj.*: bent and twisted

graceful (GRAYSS ful) *adj.*: moving in a smooth, easy, beautiful way

gratitude (GRAT ih tood) *n.*: appreciation; thankfulness

gravely (GRAYV lee) *adv.*: seriously

H

hardship (HARD ship) *n.*: suffering

harsh *adj.*: rough and unpleasant

hesitation (HEZ ih TAY shun) *n.*: a delay due to uncertainty or fear

hibernation (HI ber NAY shun) *n.*: the act of sleeping through the winter months

hues (HYUZE) *n.*: colors

I

immensely (ih MENTS lee) *adv.*: very, very much

impoverished (im POV uh rished) *adj.*: poor

inhabitants (in HAB ih tunts) *n.*: the people or animals who live in a place

insistently (in SIS tint lee) *adv.*: demanding a response; without a letup

intent (in TENT) *adj.*: determined

J

jerky (JUR kee) *adj.*: sudden, sharp movements

K

kindhearted (KIND HART ed) *adj.*: good, generous, and kind

L

lift *n.*: a device found in mechanics' garages that can lift cars several feet off the ground

livestock (LIVE stock) *n.*: the horses, cattle, sheep, and other useful animals kept on a farm

M

merge (MURJ) *v.*: come together

mineralogist (MIN er AH luh jist) *n.*: a scientist who studies the group of rocks known as minerals

Glossary

molasses (muh LASS us) *n.*: a thick, dark brown syrup produced when sugar is being refined

N

nurture (NUR chur) *v.*: support and encourage

O

outwitted (out WIT ed) *v.*: outsmarted

P

passageway (PASS uj way) *n.*: a way that one passes through, such as a hall or alley

pleading (PLEED ing) *n.*: begging

primary (PRY mare ee) *adj.*: first; most important

produce (pro DOOS) *v.*: make

Q

quarries (KWAR eez) *n.*: pits that contain large amounts of stone that can be used for building

R

reassuring (REE uh SHUR ing) *adj.*: giving one confidence

refreshing (rih FRESH ing) *adj.*: something that renews the energy of something else

rigid (RIH jid) *adj.*: stiff and motionless

rivets (RIH vets) *n.*: metal pins that go through two or more pieces of metal, holding them together

rumbling (RUM bling) *n.*: a deep, continuous, low sound that is like a soft thunder

S

schedule (SKEJ oo ul) *n.*: a plan to do certain things at certain times

sensitive (SEN sih tiv) *adj.*: being careful about the feelings of others

shabby (SHAB ee) *adj.*: old and worn out

skimmed *v.*: passed lightly over

snarled (SNAHRLD) *adj.*: knotted; tangled up

snooze *n.*: a short nap

solemnly (SOLL uhm lee) *adv.*: seriously

somersaulted (SUM er SAWLT ed) *v.*: rolled head over heels

speculating (SPEK yoo LAYT ing) *v.*: giving possible reasons for something

sprouting (SPROWT ing) *v.*: beginning to grow

sputtered (SPUH terd) *v.*: made explosive, popping sounds

stirring (STUR ing) *adj.*: arousing one's emotions

Glossary

stockyards (STOCK yards) *n*.: a yard for livestock

sturdy (STUR dee) *adj*.: strong and not easily broken

survived (sur VYVD) *v*.: lived through; lasted through something difficult

swiftly (SWIFT lee) *adv*.: quickly

sympathy (SIM puh thee) *n*.: the ability to share the sorrow of another person

T

talons (TA lunz) *n*.: claws of a bird

tattered (TAT urd) *adj*.: torn and ragged

telltale (TELL tale) *adj*.: something that *tells* (reveals) something that would not be known otherwise

temptingly (TEMPT ing lee) *adv*.: in a way that makes one want it

theory (THEE uh ree) *n*.: an idea that has not been proven

toil (TOYL) *n*.: hard work

transport (trans PORT) *v*.: move something from one place to another

tufts *n*.: a bunch of cottony or feathery material

U

unaccustomed (UN uh KUST umd) *adj*.: unusual

unraveled (un RAV uld) *v*.: took apart threads, strings, yarn, or the like

uselessness (YOOS less ness) *n*.: not serving any purpose; of no use

V

vanished (VAN ishd) *v*.: disappeared

vessel (VESS ul) *n*.: a cup, bowl, or pitcher used to hold liquids

vital (VIE tul) *adj*.: extremely important

W

wafted (WAHF ted) *v*.: floated through the air

weathered (WEH thurd) *adj*.: roughened by the weather

wisdom (WIZ dum) *n*.: a combination of intelligence and understanding

withdrawn (with DRAWN) *v*.: pulled back

wooded (WOOD ed) *adj*.: having many trees

Y

yearned (YURND) *v*.: wanted very, very much

Mosdos Press
Literature
Opal

Student Activity Workbook

Companion to

SUNFLOWER

Mosdos Press
CLEVELAND, OHIO

EDITOR-IN-CHIEF
Judith Factor

CREATIVE/ART DIRECTOR
Carla Martin

SENIOR CURRICULUM WRITER
Abigail Rozen

COPY EDITOR
Laya Dewick

TEXT AND CURRICULUM ADVISOR
Rabbi Ahron Dovid Goldberg

ISBN-10: 0-9858078-7-3
ISBN-13: 978-0-985-80787-0

Table of Contents

agriculture	feast
arid	kiln
compete	pottery
craft	rural

Fill in the blanks.

1. Hi! My name's Sam and I live on a farm in a _____ (*area where there are farms, not cities*) area in Ohio.

2. Every year, a county fair is held where the farmers _____ (*try to win*) for ribbons and prizes.

3. Since people for miles around make their living in _____ (*farming*), a lot of the contests center around plants and animals.

4. Each year we give prizes for the fattest pumpkins, the longest zucchini, and the woolliest lambs; then we all sit down to the most delicious _____ (*joyous meal*).

5. Not all the land around here is rich. Some of it is dry and _____ (*desert-like*).

6. The people who live on that kind of land compete in the _____ (*skilled work*) contests.

7. They bring the most beautiful, painted _____ (*earthenware dishes*) that they have made from the claylike earth near their homes.

8. My favorite display is the one where some of these craftsmen make their bowls and cups right before your eyes and put them in a small portable _____ (*oven for baking pottery*) to bake while you wait!

Word Families

All the members of your family are related. They are not exactly alike, but they are connected in many ways. Many live in the same house and perhaps even look alike. Words have "families," too. Here's an example: winter, snow, ice, and cold are all related. Apple, orange, banana, and grape are related, too!

Circle the word that is related to the vocabulary word.

1. **agriculture**

   piano   farming   tornado   physician

2. **arid**

   thunderstorm   river   desert   rainbow

3. **compete**

   race   write   mix   finish

4. **craft**

   thinking   woodworking   searching   sailing

5. **feast**

   fields   dough   sand   food

6. **kiln**

   fold   pound   bake   cut

7. **pottery**

   clay   glass   wood   iron

8. **rural**

   city   country   ocean   jungle

All About a Craft

When making an object requires special skill, it is called a **craft**. Tassai was good at making jars, which is the craft of pottery making. Everyone has worked at some craft, even if they didn't know it! Have you ever made a lanyard? Have you used modeling clay or even Play-Doh? Then you have worked at a craft. Some other crafts would be embroidery or needlepoint, woodworking, making a model car or airplane, or even decorating a cake. Choose a craft that you enjoy or know something about, and write a paragraph about it. Describe what skill the craft requires; for example, must you be good at drawing? Must you know how to use certain tools? Then tell what materials you need for it, and what the finished product looks like.

_____

_____

_____

_____

_____

_____

_____

_____

_____

_____

_____

Narrative Elements

Narrative Elements

Every story has a **plot**, **characters**, a **setting**, and a **main idea**. Even a one-paragraph story, like the one below, can have all those **narrative elements**. Read the paragraph and answer the questions.

The Gold-Diggers

Outside the cave, a storm was brewing. Jake and Tim sat at the entrance, staring gloomily at the dark clouds.

"If this storm is as strong as it looks to be," said Jake, "we'll never be able t' git that gold at the bottom of the creek," he said.

"Hold on," said Tim. "We didn't come all the way from Kansas to California t' go home empty-handed. That there storm'll blow itself out, and then we'll go find that gold."

"Yer right," said Jake. "Gold-digging, like everythin' else in life, takes patience."

Circle the correct answer.

1. *Outside the cave, a storm was brewing.* This tells us about the

   a. plot.   b. characters.   c. setting.   d. main idea.

   _____

2. *Jake and Tim sat at the entrance.* This introduces us to the

   a. plot.   b. characters.   c. setting.   d. main idea.

   _____

3. *... then we'll go find that gold.* This tells us about the

   a. plot.   b. characters.   c. setting.   d. main idea.

   _____

4. *Gold-digging, like everythin' else in life, takes patience.* This must be the

   a. plot.   b. characters.   c. setting.   d. main idea.

Recognize the Four Elements of a Story

Every story has four elements: plot, characters, setting, and theme, or main idea. As you can see, each jar is labeled with one of those elements. Follow the instructions given at the top of each jar.

Plot

The plot has several steps to it. Start or complete the phrase that describes each step in the plot.

1. Tassai was secretly _____.

2. The Governor of the Pueblo invited _____.

3. _____ planned to enter her jar into the competition at the feast.

4. Tassai realized she had left her jar at home, so she _____.

5. _____ followed her home.

6. While Tassai was inside, the little girl suddenly saw _____.

7. When Tassai saw the snake, she _____.

8. By doing this, Tassai had _____.

9. When the Governor heard about this, he _____.

Plot | Characters | Setting | Theme

Characters

List the four characters
in the story.

1. The Governor _____

2. _____

3. _____

4. _____

Setting

List the four settings
in the story.

1. The fields at the foot of the mesa where Tassai worked

2. _____

3. _____

4. _____

Theme

Deeds can be very beautiful, too.

Decorate the jar that contains the
theme, the main idea of the story.

The main idea is found near the end
of the story when the Governor says
that prizes were to be given for the
most beautiful things brought to the
feast. But, he says, deeds can be very
beautiful, too. He then gives Tassai a
prize for her beautiful deed.

burro	thicket
brayed	anxiously
jauntily	optimist
poncho	pessimist

Fill in the blanks.

1. If there's anything I can't stand, it's a "Doomsday Dan" who always thinks the worst will happen, otherwise known as a _____.

2. You know the type! The sun may be shining, the sky may be cloudless, but this fellow will wear his rain _____ (*a cloak with an opening for the head*) because he's afraid his new shirt may get wet in the thunderstorm that he's sure is on the way.

3. My friend Brian, a true pessimist, will spend all morning looking _____ (*worriedly*) at the sky, just waiting for the first raindrop.

4. Once, we were at the zoo looking at some donkeys and their close relative, the _____ (*small donkey*).

5. Well, the donkey _____ (*harsh cry of the donkey*) and my friend Brian, a real worrier, was sure the donkey was going to come up and bite him.

6. I, who am a born _____ (*one who thinks the best will happen*) and never ever thinks the worst, assured him that donkeys bray all the time, and that this old fellow probably didn't even have teeth!

7. To prove my point, I put my hand over the fence and waved my cap up and down over a _____ (*group of bushes*) that the donkey was standing near.

8. Was I surprised when a young donkey dashed out and grabbed the cap in his teeth! I was scared, but began to laugh when, a moment later, I saw the old donkey walking around with my cap set _____ (*worn easily and proudly*) on his head.

Who? What? Where? When? Why?

Circle the correct answer.

1. *Who* **brayed**?

   the hairstylist   the lion   the detective   the burro

2. *What* grows thickly in a **thicket**?

   berries   weeds   bushes   trees

3. *Where* do people wear **ponchos**?

   in Alaska   in Mexico   in Iceland   in the swimming pool

4. *When* are people **anxious**?

   when they are worried   when they are happy   when they are sleeping

5. *Why* are you calling that man a **pessimist**?

   because he thinks the worst will happen

   because he thinks the best will happen

6. *What* could be worn **jauntily**?

   shoes   a hat   a sock   a watch

7. *When* is a **burro** especially useful?

   when you want to climb a mountain

   when you want to cross a river

   when you want to race across a field

8. *What* is usually on the face of an **optimist**?

   a frown   a smile   tears   a worried look

Sombreros for Sale!

When Mama saw how well her white sombreros were selling, she decided to open a sombrero store. As you know, opening a store is not a simple thing. You have to decide what items you will be selling. You have to decide how to display them. You have to decide what your store hours will be. There are a million details to plan!

Write out a plan for a sombrero store.

In the first paragraph, describe the different kinds of sombreros you will be selling. Also, describe some other items you would like to sell in your store.

In the second paragraph write when the store will be open and what you will name your store.

_____

_____

_____

_____

_____

_____

_____

_____

_____

Name

Recognizing Plot

What happens in the story is the **plot**. At the beginning of the story, a problem is presented. In the middle of the story, things happen and changes occur that may solve the problem. Near the end of the story, the problem is solved.

Read the following story and follow the instructions below it.

Jean Bartlett was a third grader. You wouldn't know it though, because out in Illinois in the early 1800s, children of all ages sat in the same classroom. Those classrooms were known as one-room schoolhouses. Not all the children came each day. Some of the older boys often missed school. They were needed at home to help on the farm. Farm work was far more important than a little "book learning."

Jean was different from many of the children. She loved books. To her, nothing was more interesting than a good book. The problem was, she had read every one of the books in her house. How could she get something else to read? Jean asked her friends, Martha and Tom, for ideas.

"I've heard of a place where there are lots of books," said Tom. "It's called a library. They have one in Chicago."

"Really?" said Jean. "You mean you can just read and read and read and never run out of books?"

"Yes," said Tom, "that's just what I mean."

"Much good that does us," said Martha with a sigh. "As far as we're concerned, Chicago may as well be on the moon."

"Don't give up so easily," said Jean. "Maybe we can make a little library of our own."

The three children spent the next few weeks asking people if they would lend their books to the new school library. By the end of the month, they had an odd assortment of books. There were also magazines and old newspapers. Jean didn't care—she was thrilled to have anything at all to read. And it seemed that she was not the only one. By the end of the next month, every one of the books and newspapers had been borrowed. Several people gave their own books to the library. The "Schoolhouse Library" was on its way to being a great success!

1. **Underline the sentence that tells the reader what the problem is.**

2. **Circle the sentence that gives the reader the solution to the problem.**

3. **In one sentence, explain what the children did to make the solution work.**

THE STORY OF THE
WHITE SOMBRERO
Graphic Organizer

Andres and Francisco were brothers, yet their personalities were very different. Whatever happened, Andres was cheerful and hopeful, and Francisco was worried and anxious. In the exercise below, you will be comparing Andres to Francisco. Between each pair of monkeys there is a question about what each brother thought or did about something. Write what Andres thought or did under the smiling monkey. Write the answer for what Francisco thought or did under the worried monkey.

1. What did each brother say when Mama told the boys they would be taking the sombreros to the market?

2. What did each brother say when Francisco saw a wasp fly by?

3. What did each brother say when the monkeys grabbed the sombreros?

Compare and Contrast

4. What did each brother say when the monkeys finally went away and the boys saw how sticky the sombreros were?

_____ _____

_____ _____

_____ _____

5. What did each boy say when they saw that the sombreros had turned white from the sun?

_____ _____

_____ _____

_____ _____

6. What did Francisco say to Andres after they had all become rich?

_____

_____

_____

vision	avoid
stumble	obstacles
physician's	gradually
active	enable

Fill in the blanks.

1. Katie is an _____ (*moving around a lot*) toddler.

2. My mom is always warning us to _____ (*keep away from*) the balls, cars, blocks, and crayons that she leaves all over the floor.

3. Mom is afraid we might _____ (*trip*) and fall over one of them.

4. A person purposely setting up _____ (*something that keeps one from moving forward*) could not do a better job of testing our eyesight.

5. We always say we need 20/20 _____ (*eyesight*) to see every tiny Lego piece Katie has left on the steps.

6. We joke that the number of doctor's visits we've needed because of sprains and fractures could pay for our _____ (*doctor's*) summer vacation every year.

7. We kids have come up with a plan that will _____ (*make possible*) Katie to learn how to pick up after herself.

8. Each evening, one of us takes her by the hand and walks all over the house with her, making her pick up her toys. It's working! She is _____ (*slowly*) learning to be a little neater.

Using the Vocabulary Words

Circle the sentence that uses the vocabulary word correctly.

1. a. My father is on a diet, so he's *avoiding* all sweets.

   b. My father is on a diet, so he's *enabling* all sweets.

   _____

2. a. Remove that *physician* from the path so nobody trips over it.

   b. Remove that *obstacle* from the path so nobody trips over it.

   _____

3. a. Because she has perfect *vision*, she does not wear glasses.

   b. Because she has perfect *physician*, she does not wear glasses.

   _____

4. a. This baby is very *active*, so watch her closely.

   b. This baby is very *gradual*, so watch her closely.

   _____

5. a. My sister has an appointment with the *obstacle* today.

   b. My sister has an appointment with the *physician* today.

   _____

6. a. These goggles *enable* soldiers to see in the dark.

   b. These goggles *avoid* soldiers to see in the dark.

   _____

7. a. It took a while, but I *gradually* got used to my new home.

   b. It took a while, but I *actively* got used to my new home.

   _____

8. a. When you walk down the stairs, be careful not to *stumble*.

   b. When you walk down the stairs, be careful not to *avoid*.

A Conversation

People with similar problems will often join a support group. The members of the group discuss the challenges they face. They give each other advice and encouragement. They also exchange information and ideas.

Imagine that Valerie joined a support group of five young people who were vision impaired. What would the discussion be? Below, we have written some parts of the discussion. Complete the discussion by filling in the empty lines. Pat is the leader of the group.

PAT: We want to welcome Valerie to our group. Valerie, could you tell us a little about yourself?

VALERIE: _____

_____

JOANIE: I have something to ask the group. When people want to help me, I thank them but tell them I really enjoy doing things for myself. Do you think that's okay?

HAROLD: _____

_____

MICKY: I have to tell everyone I've been accepted to the school band. I told the teacher I do not have trouble reading music if it's printed in large notes. He told me he'd love to have me in the band. Anyone else have something new they're doing?

VALERIE: _____

_____

PAT: Well, that's about it for today. Can everyone come again next Wednesday after school?

How a Character Feels

Sometimes a story is about what happens to a character and *how the character feels* in that situation. The author may not tell the reader directly how the character feels. The reader may have to figure that out by using the information given in the story.

In the following sentences, use the information provided to choose the correct description of the character's feelings. Circle the correct answer.

1. When Debbie walked into the room, Tanya was standing on the table, screaming. Debbie looked around the room and saw a little tail disappearing into a hole in the wall.

    a. Tanya feels calm.

    b. Tanya feels angry.

    c. Tanya is afraid of mice.

2. Neal smiled to himself as he put the finishing touches on the dollhouse he'd made for his sister's birthday. "Will she be surprised!" he thought to himself.

    a. Neal is full of worries.

    b. Neal really likes his sister.

    c. Neal feels like relaxing today.

3. Robert walked slowly home, dragging his feet and looking down at the ground. In his pocket was the letter from the boss telling him that he was no longer needed in the business.

    a. Robert feels sad and unwanted.

    b. Robert has back pain and can't stand straight.

    c. Robert loves to walk home slowly so he can take in the beautiful view.

4. Tears welled in Marsha's eyes when she looked at Bingo's empty dog bed. Where was he, she wondered. Was he lost? Was he safe?

    a. Marsha is a sad little girl who seems to cry a lot.

    b. Marsha is a curious girl who asks a lot of questions.

    c. Marsha loves her pet, who seems to be missing.

Beginning | Middle | End

Valerie's story can be divided into three parts. The first part tells how difficult it was to live without seeing clearly and without knowing what the future would hold for her. The second part tells how she faced her problem and, with the help of Miss Sousa, learned how to solve it. The third part tells how good her life was with the help of her cane and the support of her friends.

In the exercise that follows, there are three pairs of glasses. The three pairs of glasses represent the three parts of the story. In the left lens of each pair, the same three questions appear.

Choose one question in each pair of glasses and answer it on the lines in the right hand lens. Circle the question you are answering.

1. What was Valerie's biggest problem at this time?

2. Who helped Valerie the most at this time?

3. How did Valerie solve her problem at this time?

Beginning

1. What was Valerie's biggest problem at this time?

2. Who helped Valerie the most at this time?

3. How did Valerie solve her problem at this time?

Middle

1. What was Valerie's biggest problem at this time?

2. Who helped Valerie the most at this time?

3. How did Valerie solve her problem at this time?

End

apothecary	miller
blacksmith	prospector
blossomed	stagecoach
furrows	tanner

Fill in the blanks.

1. It was springtime on the prairie. The farmers were all out planting seeds in the long, narrow
    _____ (*grooves made in the ground*) they had dug the week before.

2. A few crocuses had peeped out of the hard ground and _____
    (*flowered*) here and there.

3. In the town, the _____ (*a person who makes horseshoes and shoes
    horses*) was busy shoeing the horses, readying them for long trots in the warm spring air.

4. The _____ (*person who grinds wheat into flour*), though, was idle,
    for there was not yet wheat for him to mill into flour.

5. As I passed the _____ (*a person who makes leather out of hides*), the
    strong odor of leather filled the air.

6. But I had no time to dawdle; I was hurrying to the _____
    (*pharmacy*) to get some cough medicine for our guest.

7. The week before, he had arrived on the _____ (*horse-drawn coach*),
    with dreams of getting rich quick.

8. He was a _____ (*one who searches for gold*) who had come to search
    for gold. After a week out in the spring rain, he still had found no gold, but he had most
    definitely caught a cold!

Picturing a Word

Draw a line from the word to the picture that is related to it.

furrows

tanner

miller

blacksmith

prospector

stagecoach

apothecary

blossomed

What a Park Needs

Although Amanda did a very good job of thinking of everything a town could need, she left out one important place—a park. If you were given the job of planning a Boom Town Park, what would your park be like? Would you have trees, benches, and swings? What else? Describe the beautiful park you would make in Boom Town. If there is room at the bottom of the page, you may draw a picture of your plan for the park.

_____

_____

_____

_____

_____

_____

_____

_____

_____

_____

_____

_____

Setting

When you read a story, you want to know *when* it took place. Did it take place in the present? One hundred years ago? Two hundred years ago?

You want to know *where* it took place. Did it take place in New York? In a foreign country? As you read further, you want to know what *time* of day it is. Is it the middle of the day or the middle of the night? Early morning or late afternoon?

You will also want to know what *season* it is. Is it summer? Winter? Spring?

In each of the sentences below, the setting for a story is given. The words that describe the setting are underlined.

Circle the part of the setting that is being described.

Example: We shivered as the rain soaked through our <u>summer</u> clothes.

    when   where   time   (season)

1. "This castle is the one place <u>in London</u> that does not have running water," said the tour guide.

       when   where   time   season

2. The room was dark and gloomy <u>as the sun set outside</u>. There were shadows on the walls and very little light came in through the narrow windows.

       when   where   time   season

3. Christopher Columbus commanded his sailors to set sail. <u>The year was 1492</u>, and they were setting out for the West Indies. Little did they dream that they would discover a new continent.

       when   where   time   season

4. "Let's go swimming, guys! <u>The sun's so hot</u> you can fry an egg on the pavement."

       when   where   time   season

5. <u>We were a thousand feet under the sea</u>, and we watched as fish and other sea creatures swam by the window in our little submarine.

       when   where   time   season

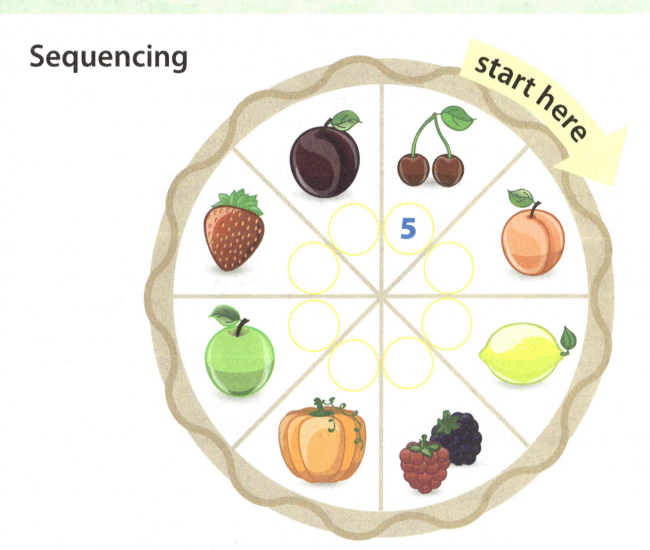

Here is a list of events that take place in *Boom Town*. The list is out of order! It is your job to put the events in their proper sequence (order). To do this, write the number of the first event in the first slice of pie, the number of the second event in the second slice of pie, and so on for all eight events. When you are done, color each slice of pie.

Sequencing

start here

5

1. Pa sells the first of my pies to the miners.

2. My brothers plant corn and potatoes and beans.

3. Miss Camilla comes to teach the children.

4. Cowboy Charlie opens his livery stable.

5. We arrive in California.

6. Amanda persuades Mr. Hooper to build sidewalks.

7. I bake a gooseberry pie in the skillet.

8. Peddler Pete opens his Trading Post.

Name

Find the cut-out page at the back of this book and cut out each picture and paste it in the correct spot.

delicacy	respectfully
dim	responsible
errands	struggled
lingering	triumph

Fill in the blanks.

1. Jordan was the most _____ (*dependable*) sheepdog in all of Yorkshire.

2. In the _____ (*not bright*) light, even before the sun rose, Jordan was up and about, running among the sleepy sheep, nipping at one, nudging another.

3. Farmer Joe also depended on Jordan to run _____ (*short trips to do some job*) for him.

4. He would send him to neighboring farms whenever he needed help with something. Jordan would run quickly with the note in his mouth, deliver it to the farmer and run right home without _____ (*spending extra time*) for a moment.

5. Joe let Jordan know how much he depended on him. He spoke to him lovingly and _____ (*with respect*).

6. Whenever Jordan returned from a run, Joe would give him a _____ (*a treat*) as a reward.

7. In the winter, Jordan _____ (*fought*) to get through the deep, freezing snow to watch the sheep.

8. For him, the greatest _____ (*victory*) was "beating" the weather to do his job.

Name

What Would You Do With …

What would you do with …

1. … a **delicacy**?

   a. Polish it.   b. Eat it.
   _____

2. … a **dim** light?

   a. Put in a stronger bulb.   b. Put in a weaker bulb.
   _____

3. … an **errand**?

   a. Paint it.   b. Go on it.
   _____

4. … a **triumph**?

   a. Cheer about it.   b. Cry about it.

What would you do if …

1. … you could not **linger**?

   a. You would hurry away.   b. You would spend time talking.
   _____

2. … you were asked to behave **respectfully**?

   a. You would tickle your friend.   b. You would sit quietly.
   _____

3. … you had to choose someone **responsible**?

   a. You would find someone who was a good worker.   b. You would find someone who was a fast runner.
   _____

4. … your friend **struggled** with arithmetic?

   a. You would offer to help her.   b. You would ask him to help you.

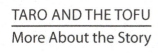

Choose a Side!

When Taro saw that he had too much change, he had a debate within himself. Should he return the extra money or shouldn't he? A debate is usually an argument between two people. Each one tries to persuade the other that he is right.

Imagine that two of your friends are debating about the lunches served in school. One friend thinks that there should be only healthy desserts, like fruit or nuts. The other friend thinks that desserts should include treats like pudding and ice cream. Choose one side and write a paragraph that would persuade the other side that you are right.

_____

_____

_____

_____

_____

_____

_____

_____

_____

_____

Name

Drawing Conclusions

Drawing conclusions means taking the information you are given and using it to figure out something you have not been told. For example, if you saw your friend packing a suitcase, you would *draw the conclusion* that your friend was going on a trip.

As we read a story, we draw conclusions. Sometimes, when we read further, we find out that our conclusions were right, and sometimes we find out that they were wrong!

Read the following paragraphs, and answer the questions.

Eric just couldn't face his mother. She had sent him to buy some bread, and here he was, on his way home, with no bread for his hungry sisters and brothers. As the cold wind blew through Eric's thin coat, his hand went to the hole in his pocket where the money had been. A tear formed in his eye and rolled down his cheek.

1. Was Eric's family rich or poor?   rich   poor

2. Was the season winter or summer?   winter   summer

3. Was Eric happy or sad?   happy   sad

4. What had happened to the money for the bread? _____

Lynn walked out the door into the yard. As the hens clucked and scattered, she started running towards the barn. She had waited up until very late last night, but nothing had happened. As she opened the door of the barn, she heard it: a soft maaa … Lynn's father turned around with a smile. "You have a new job, now," he said.

1. Where did Lynn live?   in the city   on a farm

2. What had Lynn been waiting for?   a newborn puppy   a newborn lamb

3. What had happened during the night?   a lamb had been born   nothing had happened

4. What do you think would be Lynn's new job? _____

In *Taro and the Tofu*, Taro has to make many decisions. Making a decision is like seeing two roads in front of you, and choosing to take one of them. The pictures show six decisions Taro has to make. Each picture tells you which "road" or choice was made. What was the other choice? Choose the answer from the list below and write the correct number in the road sign. The first one is done for you.

1. The tofu man asks Taro if he's sure the extra money is the tofu man's and Taro says he's sure.

2. Taro decides quickly which candy to buy so he could hurry home to his mother.

3. Taro doesn't tell his parents that he gave his candy to the sick little boy.

4. Taro stops at all the shops along the way.

5. Taro does not share his candy with anyone.

6. Taro decides he must return the extra yen to the tofu man right away.

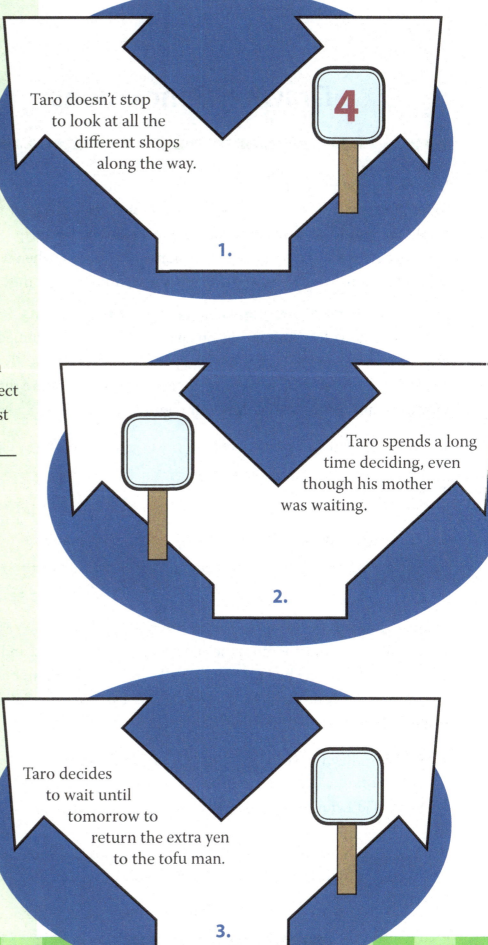

Taro doesn't stop to look at all the different shops along the way.

4

1.

Taro spends a long time deciding, even though his mother was waiting.

2.

Taro decides to wait until tomorrow to return the extra yen to the tofu man.

3.

Name

The tofu man asks Taro if he's sure the extra money is the tofu man's and Taro says he's not sure.

4.

Taro gives some of his candy to the man for his sick grandson.

5.

Taro tells his parents about his good deed.

6.

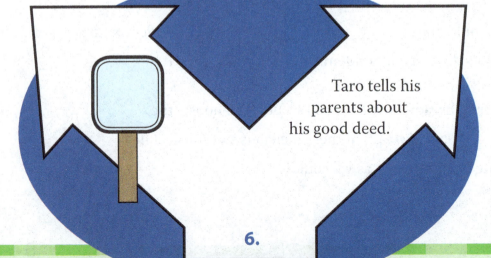

enthusiastic	farewell
aroma	foreign
correspond	suggest
despair	radiator

Fill in the blanks.

1. Pierre was from France, and you could tell! It wasn't only his _____
(*from another country*) accent.

2. No, it was also his dramatic way of talking. In America, we are not usually very emotional.
But Pierre was always either very joyful or full of _____ (*hopelessness*).

3. When he liked something, he was the most _____ (*excited and
eager*) person in the room.

4. He was so full of warmth and friendliness that we jokingly called him "the
_____."(*a room heater*)

5. Each day, when school was over, he would stand at the door of the classroom, look at
everyone, and say, "_____," (*goodbye*) as though he were leaving
for a long journey.

6. In the summertime, when he returned to Paris for a visit, Pierre would _____
(*exchange letters*) with each of us, writing long, interesting letters.

7. He was a great friend, and could always _____ (*offer an idea*)
something that would help us if we had a problem.

8. Pierre's mom baked wonderful breads. Any time you went to his house, the
_____ (*good smell*) of these delicious sweet rolls filled
the air. You can bet we visited him as often as we could!

Backwards Benny

Meet Benny, who gets everything backwards! He wears his left shoe on the right foot! He eats oatmeal for supper! And he wears boots in the summer! Could you help him, please?

Choose the correct word from the vocabulary list on page 32.

1. When Benny is really excited about a project, he says he's sad. He *should* say

   he's _____.

2. When Benny's looking for a stamp from another country, he says he's looking for a U.S. stamp. He *should* say he's looking for a _____ stamp.

3. When Benny wants to say goodbye, he says hello! He *should* say _____!

4. When Benny has some good advice, he says he wants to "command" something. He *should* say he wants to _____ something.

5. When Benny asked his friend to write him letters, he said, "Will you call me?" He *should* have said, "Will you _____ with me?"

6. One day Benny was feeling really hopeless. He told his mother that he was full of hope! He *meant* to say he was full of _____.

7. Benny loved it when his mother baked bread. He said, "I love the smell." His mother corrected him and said, "When it's a *good* smell, say, 'I love the _____.'"

8. "I'm freezing," said Benny. "Please, Daddy, turn on the air conditioner." It was lucky that Benny's father understood what he really meant. He immediately went and turned on the _____.

Write a Letter

When Jangmi left Korea, monsoon weather was just beginning. Imagine that you are Kisuni, Jangmi's friend, writing a letter to Jangmi about the terrible monsoon that passed through the town after Jangmi's family left. In your letter, describe the rains and wind of the monsoon. Write about damage that was caused by the monsoon and what the townspeople had to do to fix it. Write about how Kisuni felt while the storm raged and how she feels now. If you like, you can illustrate your "letter" to Jangmi with pictures of the monsoon.

Realistic Fiction

Realistic fiction is a story that is not true but sounds as though it is. Some of the stories you read are not realistic at all. Others are very realistic. Can you tell the difference?

Circle the number in front of the paragraphs that are realistic.

1. Maxwell Mouse peeped out of his mouse hole. "Come on," he said to his brother, "the coast is clear. Let's go raid the cookie jar!" "Hold on a minute while I get a sweater," said Morris Mouse, "it's pretty chilly out there."

   _____

2. Margaret walked outside and smiled. Spring was in the air. The birds were chirping, and the sun was warm on her back. In the garden, she could see little green shoots where she had planted daffodil bulbs in the fall.

   _____

3. The lieutenant walked up and down the rows of soldiers. Every once in a while he would stop. "Stand up straight," he would say to one. Or, "Those boots need polishing," he would say to another. The lieutenant never smiled and never frowned. He never gave a compliment. He expected his soldiers to do everything right. If they didn't, he let them know.

   _____

4. The spaceship shook. "What's this?" thought Alan. "We were supposed to have landed on Mars hours ago." Now, Mars was nowhere in sight, and the spaceship was shaking. Alan looked at his sleeping copilot Nabla. Nabla was from the planet Mercury, and knew his way around space better than Alan did. Alan wondered if he should wake up Nabla and ask for his help.

   _____

5. We had been waiting for this day to come. It was the day we would begin the dangerous climb up Mount Everest. We were all there, the six climbers and the four guides. The weather forecast was not good. A blizzard was expected. A shiver of fear went down my back, but I decided not to think about it.

GOOD-BYE, 382 SHIN DANG DONG

Graphic Organizer

Jangmi is a girl who is living through some changes in her life. She is changing her house, her city, her school, and her friends. How does Jangmi feel about all this? The story tells you what her feelings are.

In each suitcase, you will find the description of one event in Jangmi's changing life. On the "luggage tag," write how Jangmi felt during that event. If Jangmi has mixed feelings about something, write both of the feelings. You may choose your answers from the list of emotions on the next page, or you may use your own ideas.

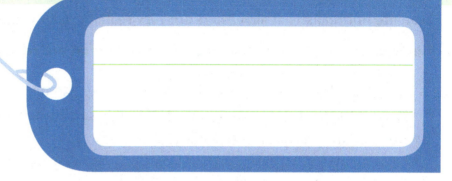

1. **I opened my eyes on the day of the move and saw my bare room.**

2. **All my relatives came for a special goodbye feast.**

3. **I looked at my home from the car as we left for the airport.**

4. **On the airplane we flew over rice fields.**

Name

1. Homesick when I looked down at my country
2. I missed my old friend
3. A little happy about a new friend
4. Very, very sad
5. Happy to be with family but sad about the future
6. Pleasantly surprised
7. Hopeful that things will get better
8. Tears streamed down my face

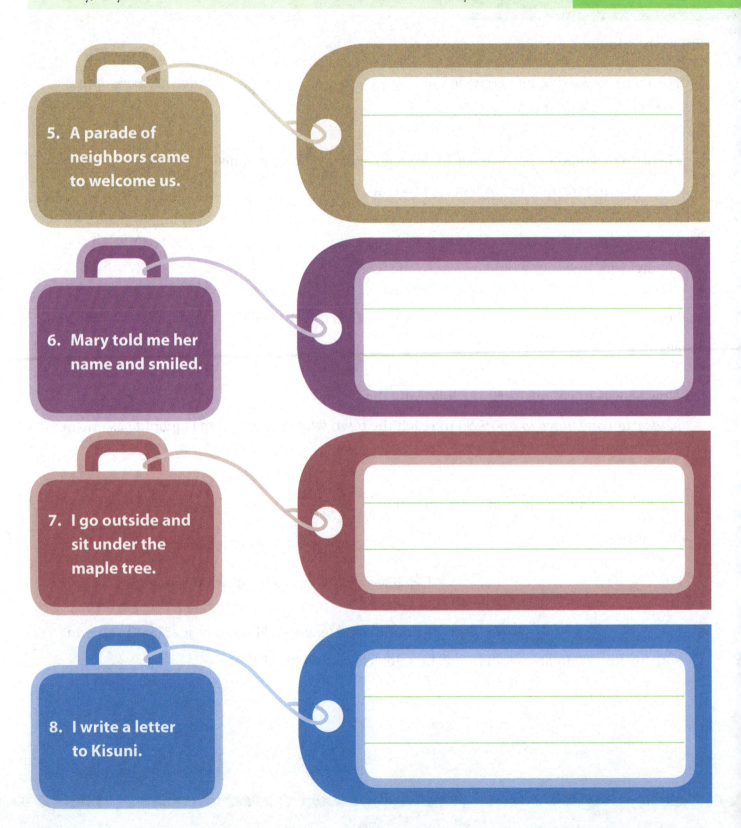

5. A parade of neighbors came to welcome us.

6. Mary told me her name and smiled.

7. I go outside and sit under the maple tree.

8. I write a letter to Kisuni.

coaxed	alerted
independence	route
strained	halted
volunteered	liberty

Fill in the blanks.

1. He hadn't needed to be persuaded or _____ (*gently persuaded*). He'd always wanted to be a spy.

2. He hadn't wanted to be a soldier in the regular army; he valued his _____ (*the right to think and act for oneself*) too much.

3. Yet, he believed strongly in the cause of _____ (*freedom*). If the enemy won, freedom would be lost to the world.

4. So, he _____ (*offered*) to be sent behind enemy lines as a secret agent.

5. Now he was in enemy territory, following the _____ (*a way that leads from one place to another*) to reach the town where he would masquerade as one of the enemy.

6. He heard a rustling noise in the bushes that _____ (*warned*) him to danger.

7. He _____ (*tried very hard*) to make out what the noise was.

8. He _____ (*stopped*) and listened. "Friend or foe?" said someone with an American accent. "Friend," he said, with a sigh of relief.

If ...

Circle the correct answer.

1. If you wanted to **coax** your horse to move, would you

   a. give him sugar? **or** b. hit him with a horse whip?

   _____

2. If you wanted to give your child **independence**, would you

   a. give her strict rules? **or** b. allow her to come and go as she pleases?

   _____

3. If you had **strained** your horses, would you now

   a. give them extra rest? **or** b. give them a good workout?

   _____

4. If you **volunteered** for a job,

   a. did you offer to do it? **or** b. did someone make you do it?

   _____

5. If someone **alerted** you, would that make you

   a. know about something? **or** b. not know about something?

   _____

6. If you took the same **route** to school every day, would you be

   a. riding in the same vehicle? **or** b. riding on the same roads?

   _____

7. If a policeman **halted** you, would you

   a. stop? **or** b. go?

   _____

8. If you were fighting for **liberty**, would you be seeking

   a. riches? **or** b. freedom?

A Hero

Sybil is a good example of how a young person did something that took a lot of courage. Do you know any stories about children or teenagers who were heroes? Maybe it is someone you know or something you read about. Write a paragraph that describes the event. If you do not know about something that really happened, you can make up a story that tells about a youngster doing something very brave.

_____

_____

_____

_____

_____

_____

_____

_____

_____

_____

_____

Author's Purpose

The reason an author writes something is called the **author's purpose**. Authors write for many reasons. Sometimes, they wish to *inform*, or tell you about something. They may wish to *persuade* you to do something, to buy something, or to believe something. They may just want to *entertain* you. Or, they may wish to *share their feelings* with you.

Below are four pieces of writing. Under each one, choose the answer that best describes what the author's purpose was.

Circle the letter in front of the best answer.

1. It is time to replace those old light bulbs. It is true that the new light bulbs cost more, but they will save money, last longer, and use less energy to run. These are the ones you should buy.

    a. To inform   c. To entertain

    b. To persuade   d. To share feelings

2. It's a warm wind, the west wind, full of birds' cries.
   I never hear the west wind but tears are in my eyes.

    a. To inform   c. To entertain

    b. To persuade   d. To share feelings

3. I never saw a purple cow, I never hope to see one,
   But I can tell you anyhow, I'd rather see than be one.

    a. To inform   c. To entertain

    b. To persuade   d. To share feelings

4. Scientists have studied the camel carefully to find out how it can go so long without water.

    a. To inform   c. To entertain

    b. To persuade   d. To share feelings

SYBIL RIDES BY NIGHT
Graphic Organizer

Sybil rode her horse all through the night to warn her countrymen that the British army was preparing to fight them. The story tells you about each stop she made along the way. It tells you when she made it, what the name of the town was, and what she or Star did at that place. Look back at the story to find out where Sybil was and what she or Star was doing at each of those times. On the lines in the circles below, write down the name of the town they reached and what happened at that time.

Name _____

Learning to Review

11:00 PM

12:00 AM
Midnight

2:00 AM

4:00 AM

astounded   intended

chaos   pandemonium

drifted   remarked

gasp   revived

Fill in the blanks.

1. "I see the circus is coming to town," _____ (*said*) my dad, as he sat
    reading the newspaper.

2. My two brothers, who were lying around "exhausted" from all of the housework they had
    supposedly been doing, were suddenly _____ (*brought back to life*).

3. "The circus?" they yelled together, "You know what that means!" Yes, I knew what that meant.
    They _____ (*planned*) to set up a hot dog and hamburger stand
    right outside the circus and rake in the dollars.

4. Each summer, for a few days before the circus came to town, _____
    (*wild, disorganized scene*) would reign in our home.

5. My brothers and their friends would rush here and there, buying this and borrowing that,
    until our entire house was full of _____ (*total confusion*).

6. And my mother, who you would think would be used to it by now, would walk into the house
    and _____ (*take in a sudden short breath*) when she saw the mess.

7. The entire kitchen was taken over by my brothers and his friends who
    _____ (*moved gently*) in and out whenever they wished.

8. To be honest, though, every summer my brothers _____ (*surprised*)
    us when they really did "rake in the dollars" and, better yet, rake up the mess they and their
    friends had made of our house!

Unscramble the Words

The vocabulary words have lots of syllables! Just pronouncing the words is a challenge!

There are four different color boxes below. There are parts of each vocabulary word in the yellow box. Find all of the syllables in the yellow box that make up each vocabulary word. Circle one set in blue, one set in green, one set in orange, and one set in pink. Then, write the word in that colored box. An example is done for you.

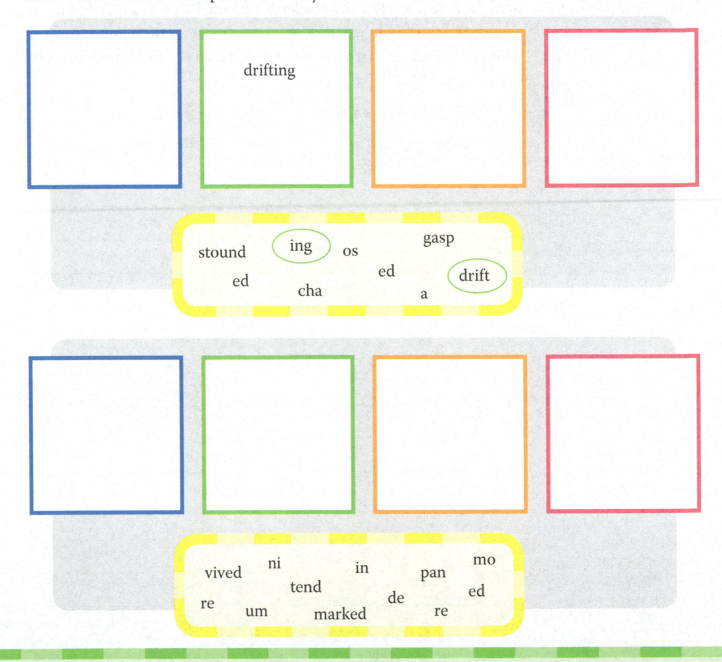

It's All Up to You!

CHAIN
REACTION

A **chain reaction** is when one event causes a second event and then the second event causes a third event and so on. Everyone likes a story that has a chain reaction in it! If you use your imagination, it's not too hard to write one. Here is a challenge for you. Below is a list of four events. Write a "chain reaction" story that includes those four events. If your story is funny, that's good, but it may turn out to be mysterious or even serious. It's all up to you!

A big key opens a door   A parrot talks

A light goes out   A bell rings

_____

_____

_____

_____

_____

_____

_____

_____

_____

_____

_____

_____

Sequence

Sequence means the order in which things happen.

Read the following paragraph.

Little Melissa dropped her sticky lollipop on the floor. Her father, who was hurrying to the car with a cup of coffee in his hand, stepped on the lollipop. His heel stuck to the floor, and the burning hot coffee splashed out of his cup onto Maxie, the dog. Maxie jumped a foot in the air, knocking over the goldfish bowl that was on the low table near the door. Dinah, the cat, leaped on the poor goldfish and swallowed it in one gulp. The parakeet, seeing this, started to screech, which woke up baby Timothy. Timothy started to holler, causing Mother to wake up. Mother sat up in bed and wondered what in the world was going on!

Circle the correct answer.

1. Which of these happened first?

    Father's heel stuck to the floor   Little Melissa dropped her lollipop

2. Which of these happened second?

    Dinah, the cat, leaped on the goldfish   Father stepped on the lollipop

3. Which of these happened third?

    Mother woke up   Coffee splashed out of Father's cup

4. Which of these happened fourth?

    Maxie jumped a foot in the air   The parakeet screeched

5. Which of these happened fifth?

    Baby Timothy woke up   Maxie knocked over the goldfish bowl

6. Which of these happened sixth?

    Dinah, the cat, ate the goldfish   Maxie jumped a foot in the air

Nothing Much Happened Today is all about cause and effect. Every single thing that happens leads to another thing, which leads to another ... Draw a line from each *cause* to the correct *effect*. The first one is done for you.

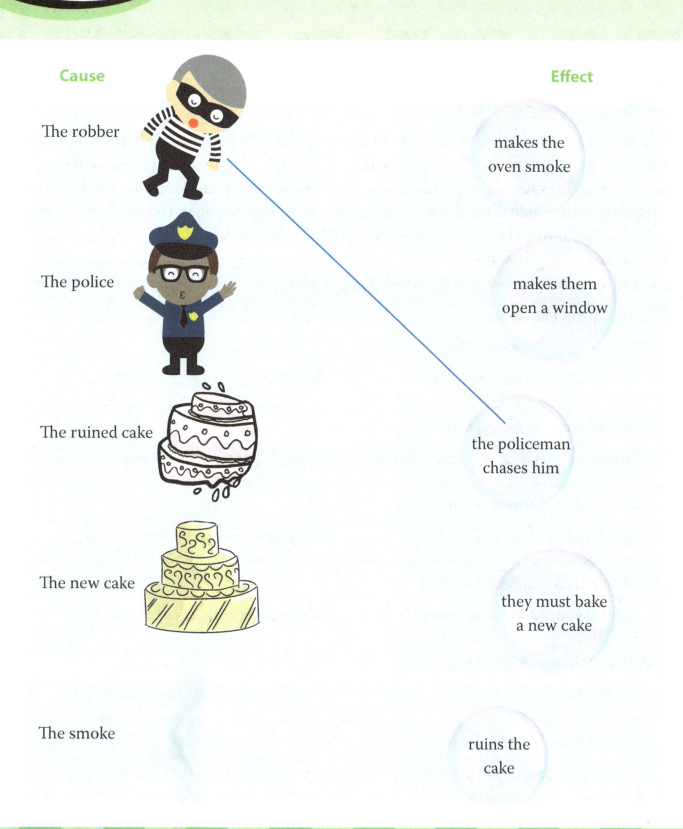

Cause

The robber

The police

The ruined cake

The new cake

The smoke

Effect

makes the oven smoke

makes them open a window

the policeman chases him

they must bake a new cake

ruins the cake

Cause and Effect

Cause   **Effect**

The open
window

is a magnet
for the dog

The cat

gets on the dog
causing him to
need a bath

The dog

produces
millions of
bubbles

lets the
cat in

The sugar bag

knocks over
the sugar bag

The bath

dismayed	outcome
dreadful	siblings
frankly	stunned
mystified	surveyed

Fill in the blanks.

1. The game was almost lost, and the coach was _____ (*unhappily surprised*).

2. He called for a time out and said to the players, "I am _____ (*puzzled*)."

3. "What happened to you? Your playing has been _____ (*awful*)!"

4. "_____ (*honestly*), I feel like firing all of you and resigning myself!"

5. He _____ (*looked over*) the group and saw a lot of really good players. What had happened?

6. He went back to the bench and sat next to his two brothers. All three _____ (*brothers or sisters*) were professional coaches.

7. Only a few minutes were left. Suddenly, the team came back to life and tied the score. The three brothers—and everyone in the stadium—leaned forward as they watched the team. What would be the _____ (*the way it would turn out*)?

8. We won't tell you, but we will say that, in the last minute of the game, the crowd was _____ (*shocked*).

Name _____

Would You …

Would you …?

1. … speak **frankly** if you were a

   a. policeman   or   b. a thief

   _____

2. … **survey** a field

   a. in the light   or   b. in the dark

   _____

3. … be **stunned** by

   a. a warm, sunny day   or   b. a shocking piece of news

   _____

4. … know the **outcome** of

   a. a book you'd never read   or   b. a book you had read

   _____

5. … call your **sibling**

   a. brother   or   b. uncle

   _____

6. … hope that **dreadful** news was

   a. true   or   b. untrue

   _____

7. … be **dismayed** if

   a. you lost a contest you'd worked hard at   or   b. you won a contest you'd worked hard at

   _____

8. … be **mystified** if

   a. things worked out as you expected   or   b. things did not work out as you expected

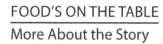

Write a Story or a Play

In *Food's on the Table*, everything happens because of a little mistake that the children make. A mistake is a good way to begin a story. Choose one of the following "mistakes" to use as the beginning of a story that you will make up. Write the story on the lines below. If you like, you may write a little play.

1. You and your sister are baking a cake. Your sister is not a very good reader, and she thinks that the bag marked "salt" is sugar, and that the bag marked "yeast" is flour.

2. There is a big box on the table. Someone in the family sees it, and, thinking it is unimportant, throws it out.

3. The doctor is seeing two patients, Charlie and Nathan. Charlie has an arm that hurts and may be broken. Nathan has a bad stomachache. When the doctor walks into Nathan's room, the nurse hands him the folder for Charlie.

Predicting

Predicting means using the information you have to figure out what will happen in the future. A weatherman is someone who makes predictions all the time. He doesn't just guess about tomorrow's weather, *he looks at the information available* and then makes a prediction. When we read, we make predictions, too. We are always trying to figure out what will come next in the story, based on what we have read.

Read the following sentences and predict what will happen next. Remember to base your prediction on information that is given in the paragraph.

Circle the correct answer.

1. "Now don't come downstairs again," said Mama. "Stay in bed and go to sleep. If you want me to bake cookies for your lunch tomorrow, I had better not see you until tomorrow morning." Ten minutes later, five-year-old Eddy was downstairs with a little smile on his face.

    What do you think happened next?

    a. Mama gave Eddy a big hug and told him how cute he was.

    b. Mama told Eddy he needed a bath.

    c. Mama told Eddy she was sorry, but there would be no cookies in his lunchbox the next day.

    d. Mama called the police and told them a burglar had broken in.

2. Sam loved water. He would splash in every puddle, and roll in every mound of snow. Then he would walk into our living room and shake his wet fur as hard as he could. No matter how carefully we watched him, he always managed to get wet and then come inside. One day, we got a new sofa. "Keep that dog away from the sofa whatever you do," said Mama as she opened her umbrella before leaving the house. "In just a few hours, the man will come to cover the sofa in plastic, and then it will be safe."

    What do you think will happen next?

    a. Mama will come home and thank the children for watching the dog.

    b. Sam will get wet and shake his fur on the new sofa.

    c. The man who is supposed to cover the sofa in plastic will be late.

    d. Mama will come home soaked because her umbrella will break.

Donald, the Downright Dandy Detective and the Mystery of the Missing Meal

The mystery:

Why, if four young ladies were invited to dinner by their very generous aunt, is there such a small supper on the table?

The characters:

List all the characters in the mystery here.

_____ _____

_____ _____

_____ _____

_____ _____

The setting:

List the two settings in the drama.

_____

_____

Name _____

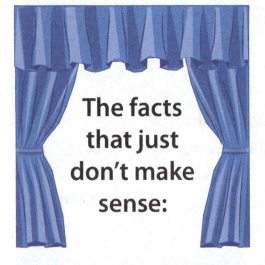

The facts that just don't make sense:

List the events that didn't seem "right" to the girls.

_____

_____

_____

_____

_____

The mystery guest:

Who is she and why is she here?

_____

_____

The solution:

What is the solution to the mystery?

_____

_____

scarcely	hauling
vast	plucking
desperate	beams
raging	settlement

Fill in the blanks.

1. _____ (*hardly*) had they set out to sea, when they spotted a pirate ship to the east of them.

2. They were frightened. They had seen pirates jumping on board a ship, _____ (*pulling off forcefully*) every bit of property off the ship, and throwing it onto their ship.

3. Even sailors who held tight to the big _____ (*thick strong boards*) of the ship were sometimes pulled loose and captured.

4. To the west, they saw dark storm clouds and black waves that would soon be _____ (*angry and dangerous*).

5. Behind them was the _____ (*a group of houses that will soon be a town*) they had just left, but there was no way they could turn back.

6. They felt _____ (*extremely needy*). Where should they sail?

7. Before them, the _____ (*huge*) sea stretched endlessly.

8. Suddenly, they saw a huge tugboat heading in their direction. It was _____ (*pulling*), of all things, a gunboat with two cannons. The pirates must have seen it, too, because, as the sailors watched, the pirate ship changed course and headed in the opposite direction.

Using Your Words

Knowing the definition of a word is a good beginning, but you must know how to use the word in a sentence if it is to become part of your spoken vocabulary.

Circle the sentence in which the vocabulary word is used correctly.

1. a. I looked at the clock. There was **scarcely** enough time to make the bus.

   b. The old horse hobbled along slowly and **scarcely**.
   _____

2. a. The sun was warm on my back as I waded into the calm, **raging** water.

   b. The ship swayed and shook in the black, **raging** water.
   _____

3. a. Having grown up in a little town, I couldn't get over the **vast** spaces I saw on my trip West.

   b. The tiny, **vast** room was so small; it could hardly hold one chair and a desk.
   _____

4. a. I was so starving; I was **desperate** to eat anything at all.

   b. I felt full, happy, and **desperate** after eating a satisfying meal.
   _____

5. a. The big engine **plucked** all the railroad cars up the steep hill.

   b. We watched the housewife **pluck** the feathers off a goose.
   _____

6. a. On our trip, we saw many trucks **hauling** logs.

   b. We walked into the nursery and heard twenty-two babies **hauling** at the top of their lungs.
   _____

7. a. The ship shook so hard, it seemed as though even the **beams** would crack.

   b. The grain was stored in big **beams** in the barn.
   _____

8. a. Anthony lived on the fifth floor of a big, crowded **settlement**.

   b. James lived in a log cabin that was part of a **settlement** on the prairie.

A New Land

The boy who tells the story in *Across the Wide Dark Sea* was one of many children who came to America. Why were their parents willing to make the long, dangerous journey to America? What did America offer that the old countries did not have? Think for a moment and write a paragraph about what made America different from the old countries they were coming from.

_____

_____

_____

_____

_____

_____

_____

_____

_____

_____

_____

_____

_____

What Is the Main Idea?

Every story has a plot, characters, and setting. It also has a **main idea**. The plot, characters, and setting are all there to express the main idea.

What is the main idea of the paragraph below?

One summer day a grasshopper saw a little black ant hurrying and scurrying.

"What are you doing, rushing around like that?" asked the grasshopper.

"I'm working hard to store away food for the winter," replied the ant.

"The winter!" exclaimed the grasshopper. "Do you mean to say you are wasting time worrying about the winter? How foolish. I spend my days hopping and singing in the warm sun."

"Do as you please," said the ant as she lifted a big crumb onto her back.

The weeks passed and winter came. Each day the ant ate a little of the food she had stored away in the summer. One day the grasshopper passed by. He looked tired and hungry.

"Give me some of your food," said the grasshopper.

"Where is yours?" asked the ant.

"I don't have any," said the grasshopper. "I didn't have time to gather any food."

"Why not?" asked the ant. "Instead of singing and hopping all summer long, you should have spent some time preparing for the winter."

And off she ran to her hole.

What is the main idea of the story?

Circle the correct answer.

a. Ants are mean and selfish.

b. Ants are able to carry loads that weigh almost as much as they do.

c. Grasshoppers have very happy natures.

d. Everyone should spend some time preparing for the future.

Every story has a main idea and many details that help express the main idea. Often, a story can be divided into sections, with each section having its own main idea. In the exercise below, the story has been divided into two. The first section is about "The Long Journey by Ship," and the second section is about "Life in the Settlement." The main idea is written on each flag. The headings in the sails

What we ate

What the storm was like

What we brought along

How long we were at sea

MAIN IDEA
We are searching for a place to live where we can worship G-d in our own way.

THE LONG JOURNEY BY SHIP

Name

of each ship tell you which supporting details you should write into that sail.

Doing this exercise will help you learn the difference between a supporting detail and a main idea.

The health problems

The work my father and I did

What the Indians did for us

How we know we are here to stay

MAIN IDEA
It was a good idea. We had built a settlement and planted crops. Father wanted to be here and work.

LIFE IN THE SETTLEMENT

exchanged   numb
fled   images
engulfed   shuddered
spewing   midst

Fill in the blanks.

1. Mike and Alec had been in the dark for hours. When the two miners had first heard the rumbling, they had _____ (*ran away*) from the falling rocks.

2. At first, they huddled behind a wall, watching one of the electrical lights _____ (*throwing out with force*) sparks and, finally, going out.

3. Everything seemed to shake until finally, the ground _____ (*shook slightly*) and everything stopped.

4. Mike sat quietly, _____ (*without any feeling*) from the shock and fear he had experienced.

5. He was afraid that he and Alec would be _____ (*swallowed up*) by the dust that had been shaken loose by the explosion.

6. The two men, trying to keep each other's spirits up, _____ (*traded*) stories about their families.

7. "We must keep the _____ (*pictures*) of our loved ones in our minds and stay hopeful," they said to one another. And so, they prayed, sang, and even told jokes to one another.

8. In the _____ (*middle*) of all of this, they heard a sound. They stopped talking immediately and strained their ears. "Hello?" yelled someone. "Mike? Alec? We're here to rescue you!" The two men jumped up and hollered "Over here!"

Word Groups

When you want to express your thoughts, the more words you know, the more exactly you can express the thought you have in your mind. You choose from among several words that have almost the same meaning, just the way you choose a color from a group of crayons.

In the following exercise, the vocabulary words have been put into groups. It is your job to add one more word to the group. You may choose your answers from the crayons on the bottom of the page, or write words you already know.

1. These words talk about the flames: **engulfed spewing**

    Another word that describes how fire takes over a building is: _burned_

2. These words talk about how people feel when they hear about a tragedy: **numb shuddered**

    Another word that describes how someone feels when hearing about a disaster is: _____

3. Here's a word that describes what people did when they saw a fire in the room: **fled**.

    Another word to describe what people did when they saw the fire is: _____

4. Here's a phrase about sharing and being friendly: **exchanged words**.

    What is another word or phrase you could use to express that idea? _____

5. Here's a word that describes something you see in your imagination: **image**.

    What's another word that expresses that idea? _____

6. A phrase saying that someone is doing something is "in the **midst** of."

    What is another way you might express this thought? _____

in the middle of   picture   conversed
sad   ran   escaped
spoke   burned   talked
shocked

Write a Letter

The day after the terrible fire at the newspaper, the fire chief went to inspect the property. He saw how everything had burned. He heard about how no one even knew there was a fire and that, if not for the deaf printers, the others would not have escaped. He was angry. He thought that all this could have been prevented. He wanted to make sure this would never happen again.

The fire chief wrote a letter to the manager. In the letter, he wrote about what safety measures should be taken from now on to be sure a fire would not start. He also wrote instructions about how to alert everyone in case a fire did break out. What do you think the letter said? Write a two-paragraph letter on the lines below.

Character Traits

A **character trait** is the part of our personality that makes us behave a certain way. A character trait can be good or bad. For example, if a boy has the character trait of being generous, he is most likely the kind of person who would share his snack with a friend who forgot to bring one. Which character trait does the character in each of these examples have?

Circle the correct answer.

1. Mr. Paulson saw the five dollar bill slip out of the jogger's pocket. He looked around, and seeing that no one else had noticed, he quickly picked up the money and put it into his own pocket.

   Mr. Paulson has the character trait of:

   a. Generosity   b. Kindness   c. Dishonesty   d. Laziness

   _____

2. "Jerry, you come here and do what I tell you," said his older sister Marsha. "Now, run home and bring me my book and some cookies. Then, go back home and do your homework. Don't go calling your friends or reading some waste-of-time book. Oh, and set the table for dinner."

   Marsha has the character trait of:

   a. Kindness   b. Bossiness   c. Laziness   d. Dishonesty

   _____

3. Mom stood at the door in her coat, waiting for us. "I'll be right there, Mom," called Terry from her room. Five minutes later, Terry strolled into the room. Mom looked at her watch. "Where's Bill?" she asked. "He's just putting his bike in the garage. He'll be here soon." Five minutes later, Bill showed up. Just then, the baby started to cry. Mom smiled at the baby to cheer him up. Dad looked at Mom. "I don't know how you do it! I would be really angry by now, and you are still smiling."

   Mom has the character trait of:

   a. Selfishness   b. Honesty   c. Laziness   d. Patience

One way of summarizing a story is through a diagram. A diagram is a simple picture that lists the main events of a story in their proper order. A diagram can also show how some of the events lead up to the turning point of the story and how some follow the turning point. As we get

6. Turning point: My father jumped onto an ink drum and signed "FIRE! FIRE!"

5. What did my father spot one day in the press room?

_____

_____

4. How did the hearing workers treat my father?

_____

_____

3. What was my father unable to do?

_____

_____

2. What did my father give me every evening?

_____

_____

1. What was my father's job?

My father was a printer.

_____

Turning Point

closer to the turning point the story gets more exciting. As we lead away from the turning point, the story begins to draw to a conclusion.

Start with number one and write the correct answer on the lines below each question. Number one is done for you.

7. What did the deaf printers do when they saw the father?

_____

_____

8. Did everyone escape?

_____

_____

9. What happened to the presses?

_____

_____

10. What did the hearing printers do on the day the press reopened?

_____

_____

11. What did the father give me before I went to bed?

_____

_____

accused	fatal
thrilling	budge
fortunately	craggy
loyal	eagerly

Fill in the blanks.

1. "Do I have to?" Danny asked his mother. "Yes, honey. If you want to go sledding, you have to take Penny along. It may not be _____ (*very exciting*) for you to have a four-year-old with you, but you and your friends will just have to manage."

2. That was the problem: my friends. The last thing a bunch of eight-year-old boys want on a sledding expedition is a four-year-old baby. But my sister was already _____ (*enthusiastically*) pulling on her boots. I was stuck.

3. We all met at the corner and headed to the sledding hill. One part of it was dangerous. It was really steep and _____ (*rocky*), so we avoided it.

4. _____ (*luckily*), there was another area that made for great sledding.

5. We all jumped on our sleds, eager to join the kids who were whizzing down the hill. All of us but Penny, that is. When she looked down the steep hill, she just refused to _____ (*move*).

6. "I can't go down," she said, as tears formed in her eyes. She looked as though she thought sledding down that hill would be _____ (*able to cause death*).

7. I could have _____ (*blamed*) her of being a big baby, but I knew better than that.

8. If my parents had taught us anything, it was that we had to be _____ (*faithful*) to each other no matter what. So, I swallowed my disappointment and said, "Okay, Penny. Hop on the sled, and I'll pull you along the top of the hill."

Name _____

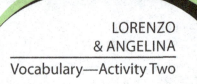
Would'a, Could'a, Should'a

Answer yes or no and then give your reason.

1. *Would* skiing be a good way to get down a **craggy** hill? _____

   Why or why not? _____
   _____

2. *Could* eating only healthy food be **fatal**? _____

   Why or why not? _____
   _____

3. *Should* you be **loyal** to a friend who has always been good to you? _____

   Why or why not? _____
   _____

4. *Would* you find a roller coaster ride **thrilling**? _____

   Why or why not? _____
   _____

5. *Could* you **budge** if you were tied up tightly in a rope? _____

   Why or why not? _____
   _____

6. *Would* you start a story about a bad experience with the word "**fortunately**"? _____

   Why or why not? _____
   _____

7. *Should* you **accuse** your friend of doing something wrong if you're not sure your friend did it? _____

   Why or why not? _____
   _____

8. *Would* your baby sister eat her mashed peas **eagerly**? _____

   Why or why not? _____

Write a Story

Angelina was sure she was right when she urged Lorenzo to keep going. Only later did she realize that she was wrong. Has that ever happened to you? Have you ever been *so* sure about something and then found out you were completely wrong? Here's a simple example. It is late and you feel tired and cranky. Your parents make you go to bed, even though you insist you are not tired. The next morning, you are all refreshed and in a wonderful mood. You know your parents were right last night; you needed some sleep! Write about a time when you thought you were right, but turned out to be all wrong. If this has never happened to you in real life, you may make up the story.

_____

_____

_____

_____

_____

_____

_____

_____

_____

_____

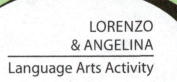
Point of View

Every character in a story has his or her own point of view. **Point of view** means the way a character thinks about what happens in the story. When you and your friend do something together, each of you has your own point of view.

"YAY!" shouted all the kids when the telephone call came through. "School has been cancelled for today due to the snow," said the voice on the phone. Mom stood there quietly. She looked around at her four children. She thought about the work she had brought home to do, and the housecleaning she had thought she would have time for. "Mom," the kids said, as they started pulling out their toys, "will you make us some hot cocoa? And then, will you make us pizza for lunch?" Mom sighed. "Of course," she said.

Whose point of view is being given here? Circle the correct answer.

a. Snow days are terrific! They are like a little vacation in the middle of school.

   The children   Mom

   _____

b. Snow days are nice, but they keep me very busy. I can't get done the things I planned to do.

   The children   Mom

   _____

c. Well, by tomorrow the streets will be plowed, and things will be back to normal.

   The children   Mom

   _____

d. Let's hope there's more snow, and school is closed tomorrow, too!

   The children   Mom

LORENZO & ANGELINA

Graphic Organizer

This story shows us how one event can be seen from two different points of view. In each of the diagrams below, a question is asked. In the circle on the left, write down how Angelina would answer the question. In the circle on the right, write down how Lorenzo would answer it. Look back at the story to find the two points of view for each event.

1. Why does Angelina begin to scold Lorenzo when she wants to leave for the village?

2. Why doesn't Lorenzo want to turn right at the crossroads leading to El Padre Mountain?

3. Why did Lorenzo slow down when he was climbing the mountain?

Name

Point of View

4. Was it dangerous for Lorenzo and Angelina to be climbing the mountain?

5. Why wouldn't Lorenzo move past the two huge rocks?

6. At the end, how did Angelina and Lorenzo feel about one another?

clammy	explored
arctic	scalding
doze	pastime
punctured	locate

Fill in the blanks.

1. Professor Lunden had _____ (*looked through something new*) almost every place in the world.

2. From the hottest part of the Amazon to the _____ (*freezing cold*) North Pole, he and his friend and neighbor, Professor Perris, had been there.

3. The professors could tell you how the moist, _____ (*unpleasantly moist*) air of the equator had exhausted them.

4. They could tell you how the sands of the Sahara Desert had been _____ (*burning hot*) to their bare feet.

5. If you named even the tiniest town in the world, they could _____ (*find*) it for you on a map in minutes.

6. Once, they had travelled a hundred miles in a hot air balloon. As they were floating above the state of Wisconsin, a bird flew into them and _____ (*made a hole in*) the balloon. They had to make an emergency landing in Oshkosh!

7. But now, the professors were retired. Their _____ (*something done to avoid boredom*) was gardening with their wives and playing "geography" with each other.

8. They would sit out in their adjoining backyards and tell stories to anyone who would listen. Sometimes, they would _____ (*sleep lightly*) and dream of faraway places until one of the many grandchildren would say, "Wake up, Grandpa, and tell us about ..."

Opposites

Circle the word that is closest to being the OPPOSITE of the vocabulary word.

1. **arctic**

   a. humid   b. freezing   c. hot

2. **clammy**

   a. fishy   b. damp   c. dry

3. **doze**

   a. stay awake   b. float   c. dream

4. **explore**

   a. search for something lost   b. travel on the road you know   c. travel to outer space

5. **locate**

   a. find   b. lose   c. shop

6. **pastime**

   a. hobby   b. job   c. clock

7. **puncture**

   a. dig a ditch   b. blow up a balloon   c. patch a hole

8. **scalding**

   a. burning   b. freezing   c. mild

A Special Day

A Day When Frogs Wear Shoes is fun to read because it is about an unexpected treat. When a parent leaves work to take some bored kids on an outing, it is something to remember! Have you ever had a special little trip with a parent or relative? Write about it. It doesn't have to be anything too unusual. Perhaps, for example, a parent took you out for ice cream after a doctor's visit. If you can't remember anything like that happening to you, you may make up a story that could have happened. Who knows, one day, maybe it will!

_____

_____

_____

_____

_____

_____

_____

_____

_____

_____

_____

Figurative Language

Do you know anyone who is *as skinny as a stick*? Have you ever been hungry enough to *eat a horse*? Maybe you passed a man on the street who was *as tall as a mountain*! If you have used these expressions, then you have used **figurative language**.

Circle the sentence that uses figurative language.

1. a. That man is as strong as an ox.

   b. That ox won a blue ribbon at the fair.

   _____

2. a. My mother says that my baby brother is a little monkey.

   b. That little monkey is cute but mischievous.

   _____

3. a. This bedroom hasn't been cleaned in a long time.

   b. It will take me a year to clean up this bedroom.

   _____

4. a. These honey cookies are really sweet.

   b. Why, she's just as sweet as honey!

   _____

5. a. It's raining cats and dogs!

   b. Look at those cats and dogs growling at each other.

   _____

6. a. The green carpet on the floor had the picture of a forest on it.

   b. The forest floor was a carpet of green.

   _____

7. a. Quick, turn on the heat! I'm frozen solid!

   b. Quick, put these ice cream bars in the freezer while they're still frozen solid!

A Day When Frogs Wear Shoes is about some kids and one of their favorite adults. Through their words and actions, we get a picture of what each character in the story is like.

The exercise below asks you to match words spoken by a character with the character trait shown by those words. For example, if someone in a story says, "I am not afraid of anything," those words show a character trait: *courage.*

Look at the box on the opposite page. Choose the quote that matches the character trait written on each lily pad. Write the number of the quote on the frog's belly. The first one is done for you.

1. **Dad: Excitable**

3. **Dad: Treats everyone with respect**

2. **Huey: Good sense of humor**

4. **Gloria: Very honest**

Matching!

1. "It's so slow the dogs don't bark …"
2. "He always introduces us as if we were important guests."
3. "Sometimes he buys us treats."
4. "BORED! … You were BORED?"

5. "We'll help."
6. "He was thinking so hard I could see his thoughts standing by the tree …"
7. "This wasn't a real hike. We came to see you."
8. "We looked for special rocks under the water."

5. Narrator: Helpful

7. The kids: Curious

6. Dad: Generous

8. Narrator: Has a good imagination

abundant	festive
ancient	generosity
boldly	panic
decisive	predicted

Fill in the blanks.

1. It was a special day in autumn. The settlers and the Indians wanted to give thanks for the _____ (*plentiful*) harvest with which they had been blessed. They had come together for a "thanks giving" feast. (The real Thanksgiving had not yet been established.)

2. At the head of the table were seated several Indians and their white-haired, _____ (*very old*) chief.

3. He was a man of courage; it was he who had _____ (*fearlessly*) invited the settlers to a feast of thanks.

4. When the settlers first saw the group of braves on their horses heading for their settlement, they were frightened; some of them even felt _____ (*extreme fear*).

5. But the man who was their leader, John Gantling, was a man who had faith in the goodness of others. They are coming in peace, he _____ (*suggested what would happen*).

6. And so they were. Mr. Gantling, a very _____ (*one who makes decisions easily*) man, immediately accepted their invitation to a joint dinner of thanks.

7. Today was the appointed day, and the _____ (*quality of giving*) of both the Indians and the settlers was clear from the many delicious dishes set out on the tables.

8. The meal was truly _____ (*in celebration of something*), for it celebrated not only the abundance of food, but also the goodwill between all the people.

Who? What? Where? When? How? Why?

1. *Who* would march into battle **boldly**?

   a. A brave soldier

   b. A frightened soldier

   _____

2. *What* would cause a swimmer to **panic**?

   a. A shark in the water

   b. Eating a heavy meal before swimming

   _____

3. *Where* would you find **ancient** furniture?

   a. In an expensive furniture store

   b. In an antique shop

   _____

4. *When* is **generosity** bad?

   a. When you want to share your germs

   b. When your neighbor asks you for a cup of flour

   _____

5. *How* does your grandmother **predict** the weather?

   a. She bundles up carefully and wears heavy boots.

   b. She knows that when her big toe hurts it always means snow.

   _____

6. *Why* are you so **decisive** at the candy store?

   a. I plan what I'm going to buy before I go.

   b. I love all the candy, so it takes a long time to choose.

   _____

7. *Who* will make a **festive** meal?

   a. Someone who is on a strict diet

   b. Someone who wants to celebrate a happy occasion

   _____

8. *Why* is the harvest **abundant** this year?

   a. Because the weather was perfect for growing crops

   b. Because the weather was terrible for crops

Important Words

HONOR

When Hamaguchi's town was rebuilt, the people wanted to do something to honor him. They decided to make a beautiful park and name it after him. At the entrance to the park, they placed a big stone that said *Hamaguchi Park*. Below the name, they explained what Mr. Hamaguchi had done for them. In the space below, write the words that they engraved on the stone.

_____

_____

_____

_____

_____

_____

_____

_____

_____

_____

_____

_____

_____

_____

Characters' Actions

Have you ever heard the expression "actions speak louder than words"? In stories, we learn a lot about the characters' thoughts and feelings from their actions.

What can you learn from this character's actions?

Circle the correct answer.

1. Bryan frowned and got up and ran out the door, slamming it hard.

   a. Bryan is worried.

   b. Bryan is angry.

   c. Bryan is bored.

   d. Bryan is delighted.

2. Debby wobbled in her ice skates onto the ice rink. She clutched the railing with both hands and took one little step forward. Then she stood still and looked behind her.

   a. Debby loves to ice skate.

   b. Debby is lonely.

   c. Debby is afraid of falling on the ice.

   d. Debby wants to show off.

3. As I looked out the window, I saw a man walking up and down the street, looking in the grass and behind the tree trunks. He had a stick with him which he poked into all the leaves.

   a. The man is looking for something he lost.

   b. The man is a spy.

   c. The man enjoys walking in the autumn air.

   d. The man is very angry about something.

4. A group of kids were talking and laughing in front of old Mr. Dinkins' house. As the door to the house opened, one of the boys, Josh, ran up the steps and offered to help Mr. Dinkins come down the steps and into his favorite lawn chair.

   a. Josh is a very serious boy.

   b. Josh is a very thoughtful boy.

   c. Josh is a very lazy boy.

   d. Josh is a good runner.

What makes *The Burning of the Rice Fields* such a good story is that so many parts of the story surprise us. Events that seem bad turn out to be good, and events that seem good, turn out to be bad. Only at the end of the story do we learn the truth about everything that has happened. In the exercise below, one event from the story is written on the roof of each hut. How did each of these events turn out in the end?

Choose your answer from the list on the opposite page, and write the number of the answer on the door of each hut.

1. Hamaguchi has hundreds of rice stacks. He will always be rich.

2. It's a shame Hamaguchi was too tired to join the villagers for the big celebration.

3. When the hillside shook, it was probably just a small earthquake.

"Nothing is what it seems."

1. All Hamaguchi's rice is burned. He is poor.

2. Hamaguchi burned his rice to save the people.

3. By not letting anyone put out the fire, Hamaguchi was making sure everyone ran up the hill away from the big wave.

4. It was very lucky Hamaguchi was not at the celebration when the big wave appeared.

5. When the people ran up the hill, they were saving themselves.

6. When the hillside shook, it was the beginning of the disastrous wave.

4. **How could Hamaguchi burn his own rice?**

5. **The people ran up the hill to save Hamaguchi.**

6. **By not letting anyone put out the fire, Hamaguchi was hurting the people, who would have no rice.**

abandoned	grace
roam	pitiful
pounce	challenge
strolled	sleek

Fill in the blanks.

1. We adopted Tiger when she was only a kitten. Someone had _____ (*deserted*) her, and we were the lucky ones who found her.

2. I'm not sure whether her previous owner had a lot of land, or whether she was just born this way, but she loved to _____ (*wander near and far*) around outside.

3. It was almost as though she thought she really was a tiger. She never _____ (*walked casually*) through our yard; she always prowled, on the lookout for prey.

4. If she spotted a bird or a mouse, she would crouch in the grass, ready to _____ (*swoop down suddenly*) on the poor animal.

5. Every once in a while she would actually kill one of these _____ (*to be pitied*) creatures. She would bring the little thing and deposit it proudly at our feet.

6. Trying to teach her not to kill anything was a real _____ (*test of one's abilities*) for us.

7. As Tiger grew into a fine, _____ (*well-fed and fit*) cat, she mended her ways and stopped hunting.

8. Her fur was a beautiful mix of browns, oranges, and yellows, and she moved with elegance and _____ (*beautiful way of moving*). We were truly proud of her.

Name _____

Understanding Your Words

What two vocabulary words would
you associate with a cat?

_____

_____

Do you know what the word **associate**
means? It means to connect one
thing in your mind with another. For
example, you may associate cotton
candy with amusement parks.

In this exercise, we ask you to
associate your vocabulary words with
some words that you know. We'll start
with one of your words: **challenge**.
Your challenge is to write the correct
answers on the lines provided!

What three vocabulary words would
you associate with movement?

_____

_____

_____

What two words might
cause you to feel sad
when you thought
about them?

_____

_____

An Animal Tells His Story

MacArthur was the first animal that Fred and Helen raised in their home. After him came Dacca, Rajpur, and Raniganj. When the four animals grew stronger and bigger, they were placed in the zoo. Imagine that one of them is telling the other animals in the zoo how he and his friends were raised in a human house. Using the first-person voice (I), write the story he would tell his friends.

_____

_____

_____

_____

_____

_____

_____

_____

_____

_____

_____

_____

_____

_____

_____

Fact—Fiction—Opinion

A **fact** means something that is true ("the grass is green"). **Fiction** means something that is made up ("the mouse can talk"). **Opinion** is something that one person thinks is true, but another person may think is not true ("vanilla ice cream is the best").

What is each of the following sentences? Circle the correct answer.

1. Independence Day in the United States is July 4th.

    fact   fiction   opinion

    _____

2. The most beautiful flower is the rose.

    fact   fiction   opinion

    _____

3. Washington, D.C. is the capital of the United States.

    fact   fiction   opinion

    _____

4. The man in the moon looks down at you each night.

    fact   fiction   opinion

    _____

5. The best pet is a dog.

    fact   fiction   opinion

    _____

6. Baby frogs are called tadpoles.

    fact   fiction   opinion

    _____

7. Tadpoles are a lot cuter than fish.

    fact   fiction   opinion

    _____

8. Lorenzo saved Angelina from going over a cliff.

    fact   fiction   opinion

Some people are born caregivers. It seems that their lives are spent helping others in some way or another. That was true of Helen. With her husband's encouragement, she helped hundreds of animals have a better life. Look back at the story to see how Helen helped each animal.

Choose your answer from the list provided and write its number on each animal's food bowl.

1. She raised them to adulthood.

2. She gave him a heating pad.

3. She rescued him from behind a pipe.

4. She bathed him and gave him bottles of warm milk.

5. She let him and his brothers splash in the tub.

Name _____

Caregiving

1. MacArthur

2. Dacca

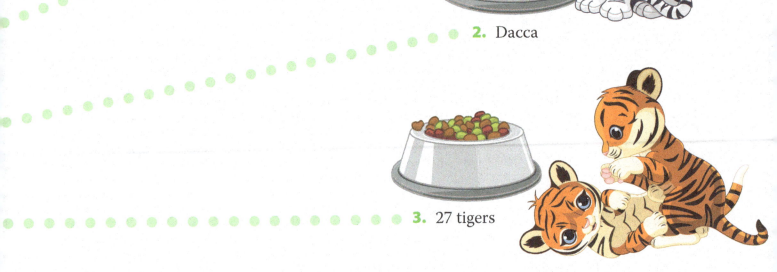

3. 27 tigers

4. Rajpur

5. Raniganj

Cut-Out Page

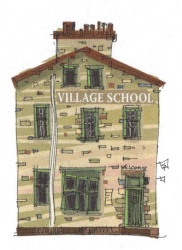

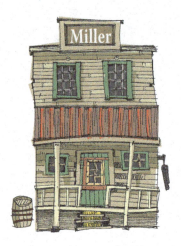

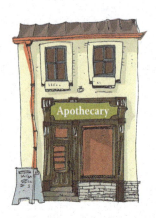

Glossary

A

abandoned (uh BAN dund) *adj*.: left to manage on its own; deserted

abundant (uh BUN dunt) *adj*.: plentiful

accuse (uh KYUZE) *v*.: to blame

active (AK tiv) *adj*.: moving around a lot

agriculture (AG ruh KUL chur) *n*.: farming

alert (uh LERT) *v*.: warn

ancient (AIN shunt) *adj*.: extremely old

anxiously (AINK shus lee) *adv*.: worriedly

apothecary (uh PAH thuh keh ree) *n*.: a pharmacy

arctic (ARK tik or AR tik) *adj*.: freezing cold

arid (AIR id) *adj*.: dry and desert-like

aroma (uh ROE muh) *n*.: a good smell

astounded (uh STOWN dud) *v*.: greatly surprised

avoid (uh VOID) *v*.: to keep away from

B

beams *n*.: thick, strong boards that go across the width of a ship

blacksmith (BLAK smith) *n*.: a person who makes horseshoes and puts them on the horses

blossomed (BLAH sumd) *v*.: to flower; to grow and develop tremendously

boldly (BOLD lee) *adv*.: fearlessly

brayed *v*.: sounded the harsh cry of the donkey

budge (BUDJ) *v*.: to move slightly

burro (BURR o) *n*.: a small donkey used as a pack animal

C

challenge (CHAL unj) *n*.: a test of one's abilities

chaos (KAY oss) *n*.: total confusion and disorganization

clammy (KLAM mee) *adj*.: unpleasantly moist

coaxed (KOKST) *v*.: gently tried to get someone to do something

compete (kum PEET) *v*.: to try to be the winner in a contest

cooper (KOO per) *n*.: a person who makes or repairs barrels or tubs

correspond (KOR uh SPOND) *v*.: to write letters back and forth

craft (KRAFT) *n*.: work that requires special skill, like weaving or pottery making

craggy (KRAG ee) *adj*.: steep and rocky

Glossary

crouch *v.*: to bend low close to the ground preparing to leap

D

decisive (dee SY siv) *adj.*: able to make decisions easily

delicacy (DELL uh kuh SEE) *n.*: a delicious treat eaten only on special occasions

despair (diss PAIR) *n.*: a feeling of hopelessness

desperate (DESS prit) *adj.*: extremely needy

dim *adj.*: not bright

dismayed (diss MAYD) *n.*: unhappily surprised

doze (DOZE) *v.*: to sleep lightly; nap

dreadful (DRED ful) *adj.*: awful; terrible

drifting (DRIFT ing) *v.*: moving gently down or away

eagerly (EE ger lee) *adv.*: enthusiastically

enable (en AY bl) *v.*: make something possible

E

engulfed (en GULFD) *v.*: completely swallowed up

enthusiastic (en THOOZ ee AS tik) *adj.*: excited and eager

errand (AIR und) *n.*: a short trip to accomplish something, like buying or delivering something

exchanged (ex CHANGED) *v.*: traded

explore (ex PLOR) *v.*: to look through something new

F

farewell (fair WELL) *interj.*: an old-fashioned way of saying goodbye

fatal (FAY tul) *adj.*: able to cause death

feast (FEEST) *n.*: a rich, joyous meal for many guests

festive (FESS tive) *adj.*: happy; celebrating some happy occasion

fled *v.*: run away from

foreign (FOR un) *adj.*: from another country

fortunately (FOR chuh nut lee) *adv.*: luckily

frankly (FRANK lee) *adv.*: truthfully and openly

furrows (FUR roze) *n.*: narrow grooves made in the ground

G

gasped (GASPT) *v.*: took in a sudden short breath because of surprise or shock

Glossary

generosity (JEN uh ROSS ih tee) *n.*: the quality of giving

grace *n.*: smooth and beautiful movement

gradually (GRAD joo ul lee) *adv.*: slowly but surely

H

halted (HALL ted) *v.*: stopped

hauling (HAWL ing) *v.*: pulling

image (IH muj) *n.*: picture in his mind

independence (IN dih PEN dunce) *n.*: freedom; the right to think and act for oneself

intended (in TEN did) *v.*: meant; planned

jauntily (JAWN tih lee) *adv.*: worn easily, happily, and a tiny bit proudly

kiln (KILL) *n.*: an oven for baking clay pottery

L

lariat (LARE ee ut) *n.*: lasso; a long, noosed rope used to catch horses, cattle, or other livestock

liberty (LIB er tee) *n.*: freedom

linger (LING ur) *v.*: spend extra time before leaving a place

livery (LIH vuh ree) *n.*: a place where horses are cared for, fed, and stabled for pay

locate (LO kate) *v.*: to find

loyal (LOY ul) *adj.*: faithful; true to someone or something

M

midst *n.*: the middle of

miller (MILL er) *n.*: a person who grinds grain into flour

miraculously (mih RAK yuh luss lee) *adv.*: as though through a miracle

mystified (MISS tih fyd) *v.*: puzzled

N

numb (NUM) *adj.*: without any feeling at all

O

obstacle (OB stuh kul) *n.*: something that stands in the way of moving forward

official (uh FISH ul) *adj.*: approved by the people in charge

optimist (OP tuh mist) *n.*: one who thinks the best will happen

outcome (OUT kum) *n.*: the way something turns out

P

pandemonium (pan dih MO nee um) *n.*: a wild, disorganized, noisy scene

panic (PAN ik) *n.*: sudden, extreme fear; *v.*: to feel sudden, extreme fear

Glossary

pastime (PASS time) *n.*: something done or played to avoid boredom

pessimist (PESS ih mist) *n.*: one who thinks the worst will happen

physician (fih ZIH shun) *n.*: doctor

pitiful (PIH tih FULL) *adj.*: causing one to feel pity

plucked *v.*: pulled out with force

poncho (PAHN cho) *n.*: a cloak that has an opening in the middle so that it can be pulled over the head and worn around the body

pottery (POT uh ree) *n.*: bowls and other vessels made of clay that is shaped, then baked

pouncing (POWN sing) *v.*: swooping down on suddenly

predict (prih DIKT) *v.*: suggest what will happen in the future

prospector (PROSS pek ter) *n.*: a person who searches and digs for gold in certain areas

puncture (PUNK chur) *v.*: to make a hole in something

R

radiator (RAY dee AY ter) *n.*: a room heater made of pipes through which steam or hot water passes

raging (RAY jing) *adj.*: angry and dangerous

remarked (ree MARKED) *v.*: commented; said

respectfully (rih SPEKT full lee) *adv.*: with respect; nicely, not rudely

responsible (ree SPON sih bl) *adj.*: reliable; dependable

revived (ree VIVED) *v.*: brought back to life or to action

roam (ROME) *v.*: to wander all around

route (ROWT or ROOT) *n.*: a certain way traveled from one place to another

rural (RUH rul) *adj.*: areas where there are farms and fields, not streets and buildings

S

scalding (SKALL ding) *adj.*: burning hot

scarcely (SKAIRS lee) *adv.*: hardly

settlement (SET ul ment) *n.*: the beginnings of a town; a group of houses built in a new, unsettled area

shafts *n.*: long columns

shuddered (SHUH derd) *v.*: shook slightly

sibling (SIB ling) *n.*: a brother or sister

sleek *adj.*: well-fed and looking fit

Glossary

spewing (SPYOO ing) *v.*: throwing out with force

stagecoach *n.*: a horse-drawn coach that carried passengers, mail, and packages

strained *v.*: tried to make them work even better than they usually did

strolled *v.*: walked in a casual way, without hurrying

struggled (STRUG uld) *v.*: fought to overcome

stumble (STUM bl) *v.*: trip; almost fall down

stunned (STUND) *v.*: greatly surprised; shocked

suggest (sug JEST) *v.*: to give an idea to someone

surveyed (sur VAYD) *v.*: looked over in a general way

T

tanner (TAN er) *n.*: a person who makes leather out of animal hides

thicket (THIK it) *n.*: a group of bushes or small trees growing closely together

thrilling (THRILL ing) *adj.*: very exciting

triumph (TRY umf) *n.*: victory

V

vast *adj.*: huge; covering a very great area

vision (VIZH un) *n.*: eyesight

volunteer (VAHL un TEER) *v.*: to offer to do something without being told